Contents

KT-437-553

Preface

The Key Facts series is designed to give a clear view of each subject. This will be useful to students when tackling new topics and is invaluable as a revision aid. Most chapters open with an outline in diagram form of the points covered in that chapter. The points are then developed in list form to make learning easier. Supporting cases are given throughout by name, and for some complex areas the facts of cases are given to reinforce the point being made.

The topics covered for the English Legal System are suitable for students studying on a variety of courses, especially first-year degree and foundation courses in law. The book also covers topics required for AS examinations.

This fourth edition has been updated to include the abolition of the House of Lords and its replacement by the Supreme Court, the changes to the financial limits on the civil track system, the changes to judicial qualifications and the renumbering of the European Union Treaty articles following the Lisbon agreement. The sections on tribunals have been rewritten to take account of the working of the new tribunal system.

The law is as I believe it to be on 1st March 2010.

KEY FACTS

THE ENGLISH LEGAL SYSTEM

4th edition

Jacqueline Martin

HODDER
EDUCATION
AN HACHETTE UK COMPANY

Orders: please contact Bookpoint Ltd, 130 Milton Park, Abingdon, Oxon, OX14 4SB.
Telephone: (44) 01235 827720. Fax: (44) 01235 400454. Lines are open from 9.00–5.00,
Monday to Saturday, with a 24-hour message answering service. You can also order through
our website www.hoddereducation.co.uk

If you have any comments to make about this, or any of our other titles, please send them to
educationenquiries@hodder.co.uk

British Library Cataloguing in Publication Data
A catalogue record for this title is available from the British Library

ISBN 978 1 444 11861 2

First Edition Published 2001
Second Edition Published 2005
Third Edition Published 2008
This Edition Published 2010
Impression number   10 9 8 7 6 5 4 3
Year   2011

Hachette UK's policy is to use papers that are natural, renewable and
recyclable products and made from wood grown in sustainable forests.
The logging and manufacturing processes are expected to conform to the
environmental regulations of the country of origin.

Typeset by Transet Limited, Coventry, England
Printed in Great Britain for Hodder Education, an Hachette UK Company, 338 Euston Road,
London NW1 3BH by Cox & Wyman Ltd, Reading, Berks.

1

What is law?

1.1 The nature of law

1.1.1 Definition of 'law'

A brief definition of 'law' is difficult, but the following are some suggestions.

1. Law is a set of rules that plays an important part in the creation and maintenance of social order.

2. John Austin defined law as a command issued from a Sovereign power to an inferior and enforced by coercion.

3. Sir John Salmond defined law as being 'the body of principles recognised and applied by the State in the administration of justice'.

4. Law is a formal mechanism for controlling society, but it is not the only mechanism; less formal rules of morality and custom also play a part.

1.1.2 Law and morality

1. Morality is what is right and wrong according to a set of values or beliefs governing a group's behaviour.

2. Morality is not fixed and will vary from one group/society to another. Moral values may also change over time.

3. Law and morality usually overlap on major issues, but may differ on other matters.

4. Murder is an example of an overlap. It is both legally and morally wrong. However, even on this major issue there are groups who believe that euthanasia should be allowed and legally it has been ruled that the withdrawal of sustenance from a person in a persistent vegetative state is not murder (*Airedale NHS Trust v Bland* (1993)).

5. Law and morality diverge on many issues. For example:
   - abortion is legal under the Abortion Act 1967, but some groups believe it is morally wrong;
   - smoking cannabis is legally wrong but many people believe it is not morally wrong.
6. Whether law and morality should be the same is a question that is debated. Positivists such as Hart and Kelsen state that law and morality are essentially separate, but proponents of the natural law theory (based on the theories of Aristotle and St Thomas Aquinas) believe that law and morality should coincide.

1.1.3 A legal system

Professor Hart gave five factors which he thought had to co-exist to create a legal system. These are:
   a) rules that forbid certain conduct and rules that compel certain conduct on pain of sanctions;
   b) rules requiring people to compensate those whom they injure;
   c) rules stating what needs to be done in certain 'mechanical' areas of law, such as making a contract or making a will;
   d) a system of courts to determine what the rules are, whether they have been broken and what the appropriate sanction is;
   e) a body whose responsibility it is to make rules and amend or repeal them when necessary.

1.2 Classification of law

It is possible to classify law in many ways. For a law student the most important ways are by:
   - the type of law (ie the matters that the law is regulating);
   - the source from which it comes; this affects the status of the law.

1.2.1 Classification by types of law

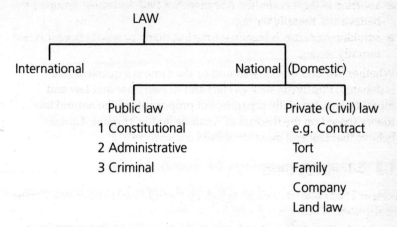

1. Law can be classified as international or national (domestic).

2. International law can be divided into public international law, which governs relationships between countries, and private international law, which governs which country's law should apply to individuals where there are links with at least two different countries. For example, which country's law should govern who inherits on a person's death.

3. National law can also be divided into public law and private law. Public law involves the State in some way, while private (civil) law controls the relationships between individuals.

4. National public law can be divided into:
   - constitutional law;
   - administrative law;
   - criminal law.

5. National private law can be divided into many categories including contract, tort, family law, company law and land law.

1.2.2 Classification by source

1. European Union law is that which emanates from the Institutions of the EU. This can overrule national law (*R v Secretary of State for Transport, ex parte Factortame* (1991)).

2. Statutory law is that made by an Act of Parliament, eg Access to Justice Act 1999. Apart from EU law, statutory law is sovereign and cannot be challenged by the courts.

3. Regulatory law is secondary law made by delegated legislation.

4. Common law is law made by the decisions of the judges. It is also referred to as case law.

5. Equity law is law created by the Chancery courts under the Lord Chancellor to 'fill the gaps' in the common law. Although equity prevails over common law, equitable remedies are discretionary.

1.2.3 Different meanings of 'common law'

The phrase 'common law' is used in a number of ways, so it is important to be aware of the context in which it is used.

Different meanings	Distinguishes it from
Law developed by judges in the eleventh and twelfth centuries to form a 'common' law for the whole country	The local laws used prior to the Norman conquest
Judge-made law developed through judicial precedent	Laws made by a legislative body such as Acts of Parliament (statutory law)
The law operated in the common law courts before the reorganisation of the court structure in 1873–75	Equity – decisions of the Chancery courts
Common law systems – those following the English case-based system (mainly US and Commonwealth countries)	Civil law systems – those operated in European countries influenced by Roman law and which are largely code-based

1.3 Distinctions between civil and criminal law

Civil and criminal law have separate functions and operate in different courts. It is important to understand the differences.

	Civil	Criminal
Purpose	• Regulates relationships between individuals • Dispute settlement • Enforcement of rights	• Prevention of certain types of conduct • Enforcement of behaviour • Punishment of offenders
Courts	High Court County Court	Crown Court Magistrates' Court
Burden of proof	Balance of probability	Beyond reasonable doubt
Outcomes of cases	Liability decided Civil remedy awarded, eg • damages • injunction • declaration	Guilt or innocence decided Sentence imposed, eg • imprisonment • community order • fine
Terminology	Claimant/defendant • Making a claim (suing defendant) • Finding of liability	Prosecution/defendant • Charging defendant • Finding of guilt

However, note that in some areas the distinction between civil and criminal law can be blurred.

1. Contempt of court in a civil case may lead to a prison sentence.
2. Orders such as anti-social behaviour orders (s1 Crime and Disorder Act 1998) are initially civil orders but, if broken, lead to criminal cases.

2

Judicial precedent

Doctrine of precedent

- *Stare decisis*
- Like cases treated alike
- Courts bound by those above them in hierarchy
- Appellate courts normally follow own past decisions
- Only *ratio decidendi* binding
- Need good law reports

Precedent in practice

- Original precedent
- Binding precedent
- Persuasive precedent
- *Ratio* and *obiter*
- Distinguishing
- Overruling
- Reversing

JUDICIAL PRECEDENT

Hierarchy of courts

- European Court of Justice
- Supreme Court
- Court of Appeal
- Divisional Courts
- High Court
- Inferior courts
- Overruling
- Reversing

Advantages

- Similar cases treated alike
- Certainty
- Law can develop
- Case illustrations of law

Disadvantages

- Can lead to injustice
- Too rigid
- Slow – has to wait for relevant case
- Complex – too detailed

2.1 The doctrine of precedent

2.1.1 *Stare decisis*

1. It is a fundamental principle that like cases should be treated alike.

2. The Latin maxim *stare decisis* (stand by decisions of past cases) is the basis of the doctrine of precedent.

3. Precedent, as operated in the English legal system, requires that in certain circumstances a decision on a legal point made in an earlier case MUST be followed.

4. The doctrine is that:
   - all courts are bound to follow decisions made by courts above them in the hierarchy; and
   - appellate courts are normally bound by their own past decisions.

5. An extreme example of this was seen following the decision in *Re Schweppes Ltd's Agreement* (1965), in which one judge in the Court of Appeal dissented. Later on the same day, when the same point of law was involved in a second case (*Re Automatic Telephone and Electric Co Ltd's Agreement* (1965)), that judge said he was now bound to follow the earlier decision.

2.1.2 Original precedent

1. Where there is no previous decision on a point of law that has to be decided by a court, then the decision made in that case on that point of law is an original precedent.

2. Usually, when faced with the situation of having to form an original precedent, the court will reason by analogy. Cases that are nearest to it in principle will be considered, though they are not binding. If there is any parallel, the court may decide that the same type of principle should apply (*Hunter and others v Canary Wharf Ltd and London Dockland Development Corporation* (1995)).

3. Such decisions used to be considered a declaratory precedent, ie the judges in the case merely declared what the law had always been, although this was the first time it had had to be decided. Supporters of this theory believed that judges did not create new law when making a decision; they merely declared what the law had always been. It is now accepted that judges do create law.

4. However, the declaratory theory still has relevance because a decision has a retrospective effect on the law (*Kleinwort Benson Ltd v Lincoln City Council* (1998)).

2.1.3 Binding and persuasive precedent

1. A past decision is binding only if:
   - the legal point involved is the same as the legal point in the case now being decided;
   - the facts of the present case are sufficiently similar to the previous case; and
   - the earlier decision was made by a court above the present court in the hierarchy, or by a court at the same level which is bound by its own past judgments; and
   - the point was argued in the case (*Kadhim v Brent London Borough Council* (2001)).

2. Only the *ratio decidendi* of the earlier case is binding (see 2.6 for details on *ratio decidendi* and *obiter dicta*).

3. A persuasive precedent is one which the court will consider and may be persuaded by, but which does not have to be followed.

4. Persuasive precedent comes from a variety of different sources. The main ones within the English legal system are:
   - *obiter dicta* statements by a higher-ranking court, eg the Court of Appeal following *obiter dicta* of the House of Lords in *R v Howe* (1987) when deciding the case of *R v Gotts* (1992) on the non-availability of duress as a defence to a charge of attempted murder;
   - a dissenting judgment;
   - ratios from decisions by courts lower in the hierarchy.

5. Decisions by courts outside the English legal system can also have a persuasive effect on English courts. The main ones of these are:
   - the Judicial Committee of the Privy Council;
   - the European Court of Human Rights (s2 Human Rights Act 1998);
   - courts in other countries, especially Commonwealth countries or countries with a common law system.

2.1.4 Law reporting

For a system of precedent to operate effectively it is essential that the reasons for decisions of past cases are properly recorded.

1. The earliest law reports were the Year Books from 1282 to 1537.

2. From 1537 to 1863 various private law reports were used. These varied in quality.

3. Since 1863 the Incorporated Council of Law Reporting has produced the official law reports.

4. There are also other well-recognised series, especially the Weekly Law Reports and the All England Law Reports.

5. Judgments of the Supreme Court and the House of Lords and some judgments of Court of Appeal are available on official sites on the Internet.

6. Judgments from all levels of court are available on commercial subscription sites on the Internet.

7. Before the use of the Internet only about 70% of House of Lords cases were reported and less than a quarter of the Court of Appeal cases were reported. Unreported cases can only be cited in court with the permission of the court (*Roberts Petroleum v Bernard Kenny Ltd* (1983)).

2.2 Hierarchy of the courts

1. a) Where a point of European law is involved, the decisions of the European Court of Justice are binding on all courts in England and Wales.

   b) The European Court of Justice does not have to follow its own past decisions. This is in accordance with the more flexible approach to precedent in European countries that have civil codes.

2. a) The Supreme Court is the highest court in the UK and its decisions must be followed by all other courts in England and Wales.

   b) Although the Supreme Court replaced the House of Lords in 2009, decisions of the House of Lords prior to this are still binding on lower courts unless they have been overruled by the Supreme Court.

   c) There are exceptions to this rule where a decision conflicts with a decision of the European Court of Justice or the European Court of Human Rights.

d) The House of Lords used to regard itself as normally bound by its own previous decisions, but would depart from a past decision where it was right to do so.

e) The Supreme Court is not bound to follow its own past decisions. Its Practice Rules require that, if an application for permission to appeal asks the Supreme Court to depart from one of its own decisions or from one of the House of Lords, then this should be stated clearly in the application and full details must be given.

3. a) The Court of Appeal has to follow decisions of the Supreme Court/ House of Lords (*Broome v Cassell & Co* (1971), *Miliangos v George Frank (Textiles) Ltd* (1976)) but see 2.5.

   b) The Court of Appeal (Civil Division) is bound to follow past decisions of its own (*Young v Bristol Aeroplane Co Ltd* (1944); see 2.5 for further detail).

   c) The Court of Appeal (Criminal Division) will normally follow its own past decisions, but has flexibility to depart from a decision where the liberty of a person is involved (*R v Taylor* (1950); see 2.5 for further detail).

4. a) Divisional courts must follow Supreme Court/House of Lords and Court of Appeal decisions.

   b) Divisional courts are normally bound by their own past decisions (*Huddersfield Police Authority v Watson* (1947)).

5. a) The High Court must follow Supreme Court/House of Lords, Court of Appeal and Divisional Court decisions.

   b) The High Court does not usually have to follow past decisions of its own. However, where there are conflicting past decisions, 'the later decision is to be preferred if it is reached after full consideration of the earlier decisions' (*Colchester Estates v Carlton Industries* (1984)).

6. Inferior courts (Crown Court, County Court, Magistrates' Court) do not create precedents and must follow decisions of all the above courts.

2.3 The House of Lords and the Practice Statement

2.3.1 The need for the Practice Statement

1. From the middle of the nineteenth century the House of Lords generally regarded itself as bound by its own past decisions (*Beamish v Beamish* (1861)), but it was not until *London Tramways v London County Council* (1898) that this rule became completely fixed.

2. The reason for following its own past decisions was that it was in the public interest for there to be certainty in the law and to prevent the same point being re-argued.

3. The ruling in *London Tramways v London County Council* had the effect of making the law too rigid.

4. In 1966 the Lord Chancellor issued the Practice Statement giving the House of Lords flexibility to depart from past decisions. The Statement said that former decisions would normally be treated as binding, but the Lords could 'depart from a previous decision when it appears right to do so'.

5. The Statement recognised that 'too rigid adherence to precedent may lead to an injustice in a particular case and also unduly restrict the proper development of the law'.

6. However, the Statement stressed the need for certainty, especially in the criminal law, and the danger of disturbing retrospectively the basis on which contracts, settlements of property and fiscal arrangements had been entered into.

2.3.2 The use of the Practice Statement

1. The Lords did not rush to use the Practice Statement. The first use was in *Conway v Rimmer* (1968), which overruled *Duncan v Cammell Laird & Co* (1942) on a technical point.

2. The first major use was in *Herrington v British Railways Board* (1972), when the House of Lords overruled (or modified) the decision in *Addie & Sons v Dumbreck* (1929) on the liability of an occupier of premises to a child trespasser.

3. However, in the same year (1972) the Lords refused to use the Practice Statement in *Jones v Secretary of State for Social Services*, even though four of the seven judges believed the earlier case of *Re Dowling* (1967) to be wrongly decided.

4. The first use of the Practice Statement in a criminal case was in *R v Shivpuri* (1986) on attempts to do the impossible, where the House of Lords overruled their previous decision of *Anderton v Ryan* (1985).

5. Since the mid-1980s the Statement has been used a little more. For example, in civil cases it was used in:
   - *Murphy v Brentwood District Council* (1991) to overrule the decision in *Anns v London Borough of Merton* (1978);
   - *Pepper v Hart* (1993) to overrule *Davis v Johnson* (1979) on the use of Hansard as an extrinsic aid to interpretation.

In criminal cases it has been used in:
   - *R v Howe* (1987) to overrule *DPP for Northern Ireland v Lynch* (1975) on the availability of the defence of duress to a murder charge;
   - *R v Adomako* (1994), which overruled *R v Seymour* (1983) on the test for recklessness in manslaughter;
   - *R v G and another* (2003) which overruled *Caldwell* (1982) on objective recklessness in criminal damage.

6. However, there are also many examples of refusal to use the Practice Statement. See for example:
   - *Jones v Secretary of State for Social Services* (1972)
   - *R v Kangal* (No 2) (2001) on whether the Human Rights Act 1998 was retrospective.

2.4 The Supreme Court

1. In October 2009, the House of Lords was abolished and replaced by the Supreme Court.

2. The Practice Direction applied to the House of Lords and, strictly speaking, does not apply to the Supreme Court.

3. The Practice Rules of the Supreme Court state that 'If an application for permission to appeal asks the Supreme Court to depart from one of its own decisions or from one of the House of Lords,' this should be stated clearly in the application and full details must be given.

4. This shows that the Supreme Court is prepared to depart from previous decisions. However, it seems likely that the court will only do so where there is a very good reason to do so.

2.5 The position of the Court of Appeal

Must follow decisions of the Supreme Court/House of Lords (*Broome v Cassell, Miliangos*).

Possible exceptions where a Supreme Court/House of Lords' decision:
- has been overruled by the European Court of Justice; or
- is incompatible with the European Convention on Human Rights.

COURT OF APPEAL

CIVIL DIVISION

Must follow own past decisions (*Davis v Johnson*).

Exceptions in *Young's* case:
- conflicting decisions;
- impliedly overruled by House of Lords;
- *per incuriam.*

CRIMINAL DIVISION

Normally follows own past decisions.

Same exceptions in *Young's* case apply.

Also will not follow where law has been misapplied or misunderstood (*Gould*).

1. The Court of Appeal is bound to follow decisions of the European Court of Justice and the Supreme Court/House of Lords.

2. In the 1970s there was a challenge (mainly by Lord Denning) to the rule that the Court of Appeal must follow House of Lords' decisions.

3. In *Broome v Cassell & Co* (1971) the Court of Appeal refused to follow *Rookes v Barnard* (1964) on the circumstances in which exemplary damages could be awarded. When *Broome v Cassell* was appealed to the House of Lords, the Law Lords reminded the Court of Appeal that it was 'necessary for each lower tier, including the Court of Appeal, to accept loyally the decisions of the higher tiers'.

4. In the cases of *Schorsch Meier GmbH v Henning* (1975) and *Miliangos v George Frank (Textiles) Ltd* (1976) the Court of Appeal refused to follow the House of Lords' decision in *Havana Railways* (1961) that damages could only be awarded in sterling. On the appeal of *Miliangos* to the House of Lords, the judges stated that 'the Court of Appeal is absolutely bound by a decision of the House of Lords'.

5. Since *Miliangos* there has been no further challenge to this basic principle of judicial precedent, except where:
   - a decision of the House of Lords is not compatible with the European Convention on Human Rights (*Director General of Fair Trading v The Proprietary Association of Great Britain* (2001), *Ghaidan v Godin-Mendoza* (2002));
   - a decision of the House of Lords has been subsequently overruled by the European Court of Justice.

6. In *A-G for Jersey v Holley* (2005) the Court of Appeal refused to follow a decision of the House of Lords on the law of provocation as a defence to murder. Instead they followed a decision of the Judicial Committee of the Privy Council. This was mainly because the panel of judges making the decision in Holley comprised nine Law Lords.

2.5.1 Court of Appeal (Civil Division) and its own past decisions

1. The divisions do not bind each other.

2. The Civil Division must follow its own past decisions, unless they come within the exceptions in *Young v Bristol Aeroplane Co Ltd* (1944).

3. These exceptions are:
   - the court is entitled to decide which of two conflicting past decisions of its own it will follow;
   - the court must refuse to follow a decision of its own which, though not expressly overruled, cannot stand with a decision of the House of Lords (now Supreme Court);

- the court is not bound to follow a decision of its own if it is satisfied that the decision was given *per incuriam*.

4. There is possibly another exception in interlocutory cases where an earlier decision made by a two-judge court can be overruled by a later three-judge court (*Boys v Chaplin* (1968)).

5. After 1966 Lord Denning argued that the principle of the Practice Statement should apply to the Court of Appeal, so that it would not be bound by its own past decisions. His main ground for arguing this for the Court of Appeal was that it was effectively the last appellate court in the vast majority of cases.

6. In *Davis v Johnson* (1979) the Court of Appeal refused to follow a past decision of its own made only a few days earlier. However, on appeal to the House of Lords, the Law Lords 'unequivocally and unanimously' re-affirmed the rule in *Young v Bristol Aeroplane*.

7. Since *Davis v Johnson* there has been no challenge by the Court of Appeal to the rule in *Young v Bristol Aeroplane*.

8. However, the Court of Appeal has used the *per incuriam* exception on some occasions (*Williams v Fawcett* (1985), *Rakhit v Carty* (1990)).

2.5.2 Court of Appeal (Criminal Division) and its own past decisions

1. a) In *R v Taylor* (1950) the Court of Criminal Appeal (the predecessor of the Court of Appeal (Criminal Division)) took the view that the exceptions that applied in civil cases 'ought not to be the only ones applied' in criminal cases.

   b) The court held that as the liberty of the subject was involved, an earlier decision should not be followed where law has been misapplied or misunderstood.

2. In *R v Gould* (1968) the newly created Court of Appeal (Criminal Division) held that this same flexibility still applied.

3. In *R v Spencer* (1985) the Criminal Division stated that there was no difference between it and the Civil Division in respect of being bound by past decisions, save that when the liberty of the subject is at stake it might decline to follow one of its own decisions.

4. Where there are conflicting past decisions, the Criminal Division will prefer the one which favours the defendant (*R v Jenkins* (1983)).

2.6 *Ratio* and *obiter*

1. In a judgment there are several elements. There will always be:
   - findings of material facts;
   - statements of the principles of law;
   - the decision based on these two.

2. Only the principles of law that are essential to the decision are the *ratio decidendi*.

3. Statements of principles of law that are not relevant to the decision are *obiter dicta*.

4. Cross defines *ratio decidendi* as 'any rule expressly or impliedly treated by the judge as a necessary step in reaching his conclusion'.

5. Zander defines *ratio decidendi* as 'a proposition of law which decides the case, in the light or in the context of the material facts'.

6. Discovering the *ratio decidendi* of a case is not always easy, for many reasons:
   - it is hardly ever stated expressly;
   - in appellate courts there may be more than one judgment with different ratios;
   - in extreme cases it may even be impossible to find the ratio (*Central Asbestos Co Ltd v Dodd* (1973)).

7. Although the ratio is given in the judgment of the first case, it is to a great extent determined by the court in a later case. It may be enlarged by being applied to a wider situation, or restricted by being confined to a narrow scope.

8. *Obiter dicta* can be persuasive (*High Trees* case (1947)).

2.7 Distinguishing

1. Where a judge considers that the material facts of the present case are sufficiently different from an earlier case, he is distinguishing the case and may refuse to follow the earlier decision (*Merritt v Merritt* (1971), *Balfour v Balfour* (1919)).

2. Distinguishing is a major factor in allowing the doctrine of precedent to remain flexible.

3. Decisions that are questionable or unpopular may be restricted to a narrow area by distinguishing.

2.8 Advantages and disadvantages of precedent

It is important to realise that for nearly all the factors that can be given as an advantage there is also a disadvantage.

2.8.1 Advantages

1. It serves the interests of justice and fairness as similar cases are seen to be treated in a similar way.

2. It creates certainty in the law and allows lawyers to advise clients on the probable outcome of a case.

3. There is opportunity for the law to develop and change with society (*Herrington v British Railways Board* (1972)).

4. As decisions are based on real cases there are practical illustrations of the law.

5. It is a time-saving device, as for most situations there is an existing solution.

2.8.2 Disadvantages

1. The doctrine as applied in the English legal system is too rigid. This mainly stems from two factors:
   - the House of Lords was reluctant to use the Practice Statement, but the Supreme Court may be more flexible; and
   - the Court of Appeal is bound to follow decisions of the Supreme Court/House of Lords.

2. This rigidity can create injustice in an individual case.

3. The law is slow to develop; it is recognised that areas of law are unclear and in need of reform, but changes cannot be made unless a case on the particular point of law comes before the court.

4. The law is complex, with too many fine distinctions.

5. The large number of reported cases make it difficult to find the relevant law.

2.9 The judicial role in precedent

1. Large areas of law have been developed by the judges, for example rules on formation of contracts, the tort of negligence and the meaning of 'intention' in criminal law.

2. The right of judges to create and/or reform law is unconstitutional as judges are not our elected law-makers.

3. The development of the law can depend on whether the judge is an active or passive law-maker.

4. Active law-making can be seen in *R v R* (1991), where the House of Lords ruled that there was a crime of marital rape.

5. Passive law-making is illustrated by *C v DPP* (1995), where the House of Lords refused to change a common law presumption about the criminal responsibility of children under the age of 14, stating that it was for Parliament to make such changes.

3

Legislation

Acts of Parliament

- Pressure for legislation
- Consultation
- Green and White Papers
- Drafting process
- Passage through Parliament
- Coming into force

LEGISLATION

Delegated legislation

- Types
  - a) Orders in Council
  - b) Statutory instruments
  - c) By-laws
- Need for delegated legislation
- Control by Parliament
- Control by the courts

Statutory interpretation

- Literal v purposive approach
- Literal, Golden and Mischief Rules
- Intrinsic and extrinsic aids
- Rules of language
- Presumptions

3.1 Acts of Parliament

About 70 to 80 Acts of Parliament are passed each year. In addition there is a considerable amount of delegated legislation each year, including over 3,000 statutory instruments. If a legislative provision is not clear then the judges have to interpret it in order to apply it.

3.1.1 Pre-parliamentary process and consultation

1. Pressure for new laws comes from a variety of sources. The main ones are:
   - Government policy;
   - EU Law;
   - Law Commission reports;
   - reports by other commissions or committees;
   - pressure groups.

2. The Government sets out its legislative programme for the parliamentary session in the Queen's Speech at the opening of Parliament.

3. Usually the government department responsible for the projected legislation will decide whether to consult prior to issuing a Green Paper.

4. *Making the Law* (1992), a Report by the Hansard Society, emphasised the need for consultation. It pointed out that the lack of consultation could lead to last-minute changes in Bills as they went through Parliament, as happened with the Broadcasting Bill 1989.

5. Consultation has become more common in recent years.

6. The Law Commission has a duty to review areas of law and will research and consult before drawing up proposals for reform.

7. Some Bills may be the result of reports by other committees or commissions, which will have heard evidence about the issues concerned.

3.1.2 Green and White Papers

1. A Green Paper sets out the tentative proposals for changes to the law and invites comments.

2. Green Papers were first used in 1967 and are now usually used as part of the legislative process.

3. A White Paper is a firm proposal for a new law. Sometimes there may be a draft Bill annexed to the White Paper.

3.1.3 The drafting process

1. A draft Act is called a Bill.

2. The vast majority of Bills are introduced by the Government of the day. These Government Bills are drafted by parliamentary counsel to the Treasury.

3. The government department responsible for the legislation will give detailed instructions to the parliamentary counsel.

4. The Renton Committee, in *Preparation of Legislation* (1975), criticised the quality of draftsmanship. The four main criticisms were:
   - the language used in statutes was obscure and complex;
   - over-elaboration in an effort to obtain certainty;
   - illogical and unhelpful structure;
   - amendment of previous Acts by later Acts making it difficult to discover the current law.

5. Since 1998 there must be a written statement that the Bill is compatible with the European Convention on Human Rights. Alternatively, the Government can say that no such statement could be made but that it wishes to proceed with the Bill.

3.2 The process in Parliament

Each Bill goes through a number of stages before it becomes an Act. If the Bill is voted against at the Second Reading or Third Reading in either House then it does not become law.

3.2.1 Introducing a Bill to Parliament

1. Bills can be introduced into Parliament in the House of Commons or the House of Lords.

2. Government Bills are introduced by the Government through the relevant minister; such Bills are known as Government Bills and will almost always become law as the Government usually has a majority in the House of Commons.

3. A Private Member's Bill is one which is introduced by a backbench MP. There are three ways in which this can be done:
   - drawing a position in the ballot held in each Parliamentary session;
   - under Standing Order No 39;
   - under the ten-minute rule (Standing Order No 10).

4. The time in Parliament for Private Members' Bills is very limited. Unless the Bill is supported by the Government it only has a small chance of becoming law.

3.2.2 Types of Bill

1. Public Bill – one which relates to matters that affect the general public; most Government Bills will be Public Bills.

2. Private Bill – one which relates to the powers and interests of certain private individuals or institutions (eg University College London Act 1996). The procedure for a Private Bill is slightly different to that for a Public Bill, with the Committee stage being the most important aspect, while the Second and Third Readings are more of a formality.

3. Hybrid Bill – one with features of both a Public and a Private Bill (eg Channel Tunnel Bill 1986–87).

3.2.3 Passing a Bill

A Bill may be started in either the House of Commons or the House of Lords, but it has to go through the same procedure in each House and pass all stages of the legislative process in order to become law.

1. First Reading – a formality at which the title of the Bill is read out and a day named for the Second Reading.

2. Second Reading – the main debate on the principles of the Bill.

3. Committee Stage – a consideration of each clause of the Bill.

4. Report Stage – a report to the whole House of amendments proposed by the Committee stage.

5. Third Reading – the final vote on the Bill; there will be a further debate about the Bill only if at least six members request it.

6. The other house – if the Bill started in the House of Commons, then the above five stages are carried out in the House of Lords, and vice versa.

7. Royal Assent – a formal assent to the Bill by the Monarch. The Bill is now an Act of Parliament.

3.2.4 The Parliament Acts 1911 and 1949

1. The House of Lords' power to prevent Bills from becoming law is limited by these Acts.

2. For a 'Money Bill' that has been passed by the House of Commons, the Government may choose to re-introduce that Bill after one month and, if it passes the House of Commons for a second time, it then becomes law.

3. For all other Bills the delay time is one year.

4. The House of Commons very rarely uses the power under the Parliament Acts (eg War Crimes Act 1991, Hunting Act 2004).

5. Where a Bill has been started in the House of Lords but has been voted against, it cannot be re-introduced.

3.2.5 Coming into force

1. An Act of Parliament comes into force on:
   - the commencement date (if any) given in the Act; or
   - the date set by the appropriate Government Minister if there is an 'appointed day' section; or
   - midnight following the Royal Assent if there is no indication in the Act.

2. There is much criticism of the use of appointed day sections, where different parts of the Act may be brought into effect at different times. This makes it difficult to discover whether a certain provision is in force or not.

3. Some sections may never be brought into force, bringing into question why they were enacted in the first place.

3.3 Advantages of statute law over case law

1. There is the opportunity for consultation.

2. Law can be passed to avoid future problems.

3. The change to the law is usually prospective, thus not affecting existing contracts, etc. However, a few Acts have been made retrospective (War Damage Act 1965, War Crimes Act 1991).

4. The law is known in advance, rather than after the judgment in a case.

5. An Act can cover a wide range of points.

6. Statutory law supersedes common law.

7. It cannot normally be challenged because of the sovereignty of Parliament.

3.4 Parliamentary sovereignty

1. No challenge can normally be made to an Act of Parliament.

2. This is so even if the Act is unreasonable or if it was produced by fraud (*British Railways Board v Pickin* (1974)).

3. However, where an Act is in conflict with European Union legislation, then the EU law takes priority (*Factortame case No 1* (1989) and *No 2* (1991)).

4. a) Since 2000, where an Act of Parliament is incompatible with the European Convention on Human Rights the court may make a declaration of incompatibility.

   b) This does not invalidate the Act; it simply draws the Government's attention to the problem and the Government can choose whether or not to amend the Act.

   c) In 2004 the House of Lords held that the Anti-Terrorism, Crime and Security Act 2001 was incompatible with human rights legislation. The Government then changed the law by passing the Prevention of Terrorism Act 2005.

3.5 Delegated legislation

Delegated legislation is law made by a body other than Parliament, but with Parliament's authority. That authority is given in a parent or enabling Act.

3.5.1 Types of delegated legislation

1. Orders in Council – made by the Queen and Privy Council. These can be made when Parliament is not sitting, under the with Civil Contingencies Act 2004. There is also power to give effect to EU law under the European Communities Act 1972.

2. Statutory instruments – made by Government Ministers. This is the most used type of delegated legislation.

3. Local authority by-laws – made by local councils in respect of matters in their area.

4. By-laws made by public corporations – made to regulate behaviour in such areas as London Underground.

5. Court rules – made by Court Rules Committees in respect of the various courts and their procedures.

3.5.2 Need for delegated legislation

1. There is a lack of parliamentary time for considering all necessary regulations.

2. It allows more detail to be included than is possible in an Act of Parliament.

3. There is expertise for matters requiring technical knowledge.

4. There is local knowledge for local by-laws.

5. It allows more time for consultation.

6. It is easier to amend than an Act of Parliament.

3.5.3 Control of delegated legislation

Parliamentary	Judicial
Enabling Act sets parameters	Can be challenged in the courts under the doctrine of *ultra vires*
Affirmative resolution requires parliamentary vote	This can be: • substantive; or • procedural
Negative resolution allows a debate to be requested	If found to be *ultra vires* the legislation can be declared void
Delegated Powers Scrutiny Committee reports to House of Lords	
Joint Select Committee reviews statutory instruments	
Ministers can be questioned	

1. Parliament sets the parameters for the delegated legislation in the enabling Act.

2. The House of Lords' Delegated Powers Scrutiny Committee (set up in 1993) considers whether the provisions of Bills give inappropriate delegated legislative power. It reports to the House of Lords before the Committee Stage on the Bill.

3. The Joint Select Committee on Statutory Instruments reviews all statutory instruments and draws the attention of both Houses of Parliament to points that need to be considered. The main reasons for referring a statutory instrument to Parliament are:
   - it imposes a tax;
   - it has retrospective effect;
   - it has gone beyond the powers given in the enabling Act;
   - it makes unusual or unexpected use of the powers;
   - it is unclear or defective in some way.

4. A few statutory instruments have to be considered and approved by Parliament under the affirmative resolution procedure. The enabling Act specifies where this is required.

5. Most statutory instruments are subject to the negative resolution procedure. This means that they will become law within 40 days unless a debate is requested by an MP.

6. If a statutory instrument (SI) is made under the power given in the Legislative and Regulatory Reform Act 2006 it can be subject to:
   - a super affirmative resolution; or
   - an affirmative resolution; or
   - a negative resolution.

7. A super affirmative resolution means that, as well as both Houses voting on the SI, the Minister whose department issued the SI must have regard to:
   - any representations by those consulted on the SI;
   - any resolution of either House of Parliament;
   - any recommendations by a committee of either House of Parliament which was asked to report on the draft order.

8. MPs may question the relevant Minister in Parliament about proposed delegated legislation.

9. The courts can declare void any delegated legislation which goes beyond the maker's powers, under the doctrine of *ultra vires*. (See, for

example, *R v Home Secretary, ex parte Fire Brigades Union* (1995), *R v Secretary of State for Education and Employment, ex parte National Union of Teachers* (2002)).

10. Delegated legislation can also be declared *ultra vires* because the correct procedures were not followed (*Aylesbury Mushroom case* (1972)).

3.5.4 Disadvantages of delegated legislation

1. It is undemocratic as most regulations are made by civil servants or other unelected people, except for local authority by-laws which are made by an elected council.

2. 'Henry VIII' clauses can give power to delegated legislation to amend or repeal Acts of Parliament.

3. There is inadequate parliamentary control.

4. There is a lack of publicity.

5. There are too many regulations through delegated legislation.

3.6 Statutory interpretation

A large percentage of cases heard by the House of Lords and the Court of Appeal (Civil Division) involve the meanings of words in a statute or delegated legislation.

3.6.1 Need for statutory interpretation

1. Words are an imperfect means of communication.

2. There may be ambiguity – words often have more than one meaning.

3. A broad term may have been used which is not clear (*Brock v DPP* (1993) on the meaning of 'type' in the Dangerous Dogs Act 1991).

4. There may have been a drafting error or omission.

5. New developments can lead to words not covering present-day situations (*Royal College of Nursing v DHSS* (1981)).

3.6.2 Approaches to statutory interpretation

There is a major debate as to whether judges should interpret legislation so as to give effect to the intention or purpose of that legislation (purposive approach), or whether judges should take the words at their literal meaning (literal approach).

Literal approach

1. The literal approach gives words their plain, ordinary, dictionary meaning.

2. The literal approach is preferred by 'conservative' judges who do not believe that a judge's role is to create law.

Purposive approach

3. The purposive approach is a broader approach. Judges try to decide what Parliament was trying to achieve.

4. The purposive approach is the one favoured by activist or creative judges, such as Lord Denning.

European approach

5. The European approach to interpretation is based on the purposive approach.

6. As a result of the European influence, our courts are becoming more likely to use the purposive approach.

Comment

7. Since any of the rules or approaches can be used, it is sometimes suggested that judges simply use the rule that will give them the result they want in the case.

8. This can possibly be seen in the decision of Lord Parker in *Smith v Hughes* (1960). Lord Parker normally supported the literal approach. However, in *Smith v Hughes* he ignored the literal wording of the Act but pointed out that the Street Offences Act 1959 was passed in order to prevent prostitutes soliciting men who were on the streets.

3.6.3 Rules of interpretation

The courts developed three 'rules': the Literal Rule, the Golden Rule and the Mischief Rule, for statutory interpretation. These rules have now largely been superseded by the literal versus purposive approaches, but even so they are sometimes used.

1. Literal Rule – this uses the plain, ordinary, literal, grammatical meaning of the words (*Whiteley v Chappell* (1868), *London and North Eastern Railway Co v Berriman* (1946), *Lees v Secretary of State for Social Services* (1985)).

   ■ Where words have a technical legal meaning then, under the Literal Rule, this will be used (*Fisher v Bell* (1960)).

   ■ 'If the words of an Act are clear, then you must follow them, even though they lead to a manifest absurdity' (*Lord Esher in R v Judge of the City of London Court* (1892)).

2. Golden Rule – this is a modification of the Literal Rule, where the literal interpretation would lead to an absurdity. Zander has described this rule as 'an unpredictable safety-valve to permit the courts to escape from some of the more unpalatable effects of the literal rule'.

3. There are two ways in which the Golden Rule has operated in cases:

   ■ the narrow application, where words are capable of having more than one meaning, in which case the meaning that is least absurd should be used (*R v Allen* (1872));

   ■ the wider application, which is used to modify words to avoid an absurdity (*Adler v George* (1964)) or to avoid a repugnant situation (*Re Sigsworth* (1935)).

4. Mischief Rule – this was first formulated in *Heydon's case* (1584). The court looks to see what gap or 'mischief' in the law the Act was passed to cover (*Smith v Hughes* (1960)).

3.6.4 Intrinsic aids

1. Intrinsic aids are those other parts of the Act which may help to make the meaning of the particular section clear. These are:

   ■ the long title and the short title;
   ■ the preamble, if any;
   ■ definition sections;
   ■ schedules;
   ■ headings before any section or groups of sections.

2. Marginal notes are not generally accepted as an intrinsic aid, as they are not part of the Act as voted on by Parliament but are added at the printing stage.

3.6.5 Extrinsic aids

1. These are matters outside the Act in question which may be considered by the courts. Extrinsic aids that are fully accepted are:
   - dictionaries;
   - historical setting;
   - previous Acts of Parliament;
   - earlier case law.

2. Reference to *Hansard* is now allowed, but only where:
   - the legislation is ambiguous or obscure; and
   - the material relied on consists of statements made by a Minister or other promoter of the Bill; and
   - the statements relied on are clear.

3. Where the court is interpreting law that was passed to give effect to an international Convention or a European Directive, then *Hansard* can be used more widely. The court may consider ministerial statements even if the statute does not appear to be ambiguous or obscure (*Three Rivers District Council and others v Bank of England (No 2)* (1996)).

4. Law reform reports by bodies such as the Law Commission may be considered, but only to discover the 'mischief' or gap in the law with which the legislation based on the report was designed to deal (*Black Clawson case* (1975)). However, in *R v G and another* (2003) the House of Lords considered the Law Commission's Report which led to the passing of the Criminal Damage Act 1971, pointing out that the meaning of 'reckless' was made plain in it.

5. International Conventions and any *travaux préparatoires* material issued in relation to the convention may be considered when considering the meaning of English legislation based on the Convention (*Fothergill v Monarch Airlines Ltd* (1980)).

3.6.6 Rules of language

These are rules to aid interpreting certain formats of words. If the particular format is not used then the rule has no relevance. The rules are:
   - *ejusdem generis* – where a list of words is followed by general words, then the general words are limited to the same kind of items as those in the list (*Powell v Kempton Park Race Course* (1899));
   - *expressio unius est exclusio alterius* – the mention of one thing excludes another. Where there is a list of words which is not followed by

general words then the Act applies only to the items in the list
(*Tempest v Kilner* (1846));

■ *noscitur a sociis* – a word is known by the company it keeps. Words
must be looked at in their context (*Inland Revenue Commissioners v
Frere* (1965)).

3.6.7 Presumptions

The courts will make certain presumptions about the law, but these are
only a starting point. If the Act expressly or by implication states that the
presumption will not apply, then it does not. The main presumptions are:

■ against a change to the common law;
■ that *mens rea* is required;
■ the Crown is not bound unless the statute expressly says so;
■ Parliament did not intend to oust the jurisdiction of the courts;
■ legislation does not apply retrospectively.

3.6.8 The European approach

1. The purposive approach to interpretation is favoured by most
   European legal systems. Consequently, the European Court of Justice
   takes this approach.

2. In *Henn and Derby v DPP* (1981) Lord Diplock contrasted this with the
   English courts' approach, saying that the European Court of Justice
   'seeks to give effect to what it perceives to be the spirit rather than the
   letter of the Treaties'.

3. The Treaty of Rome requires Member States to 'take all appropriate
   measures . . . to ensure the fulfilment of the obligations' under the
   Treaty. This encourages the courts in Member States to use the purposive approach.

4. Where a European Directive has been issued 'national courts are
   required to interpret their national law in the light of the wording and
   the purpose of the directive' (*von Colson v Land Nordrhein-Westfalen*
   (1984)).

5. As a result, when deciding points of law that involve European law, the
   English courts are using the purposive approach.

6. There has also been a gradual move towards a greater use of the
   purposive approach in other cases before the English courts (*Pepper v
   Hart* (1993)).

3.6.9 The effect of the Human Rights Act 1998

1. Section 3 of the Human Rights Act 1998 requires courts in England and Wales, as far as is possible, to read and give effect to legislation in a way which is compatible with the rights in the European Convention on Human Rights.

2. This has been done in a number of cases; eg in *Attorney-General's Reference No 4 of 2002* (2004) the House of Lords held that s11 of the Terrorism Act 2000 could be read as imposing an evidential burden rather than a legal burden regarding the defendant proving he was not a member of a proscribed terrorist group.

3. In some cases the courts have given very wide interpretations in order to comply with the Convention; eg in *Ghaidan v Godin-Mendoza* (2002) it was held that the words in the Rent Act 1977 'as his or her wife or husband' could be read as meaning 'as if they were his or her wife or husband', in order to comply with the Convention rights in respect of sexual discrimination and give protection to same-sex relationships.

3.6.10 The judicial role in interpretation

1. Traditionalist judges favour the passive role in interpretation, believing that they should apply the law as shown by the words, and not 'fill in the gaps' in legislation.

2. This view was expressed by Viscount Dilhorne: 'If language is clear and explicit, the court must give effect to it, for in that case the words of the state speak for the intention of the legislature' (*Kammins Ballroom Co Ltd v Zenith Investments Ltd* (1970)).

3. Activist judges favour the purposive approach to interpretation and see their role as a more creative one.

4. Lord Denning was a major supporter of the activist role: 'We sit here to find out the intention of Parliament and carry it out, and we do this better by filling in the gaps and making sense of the enactment than by opening it up to destructive analysis' (*Magor and St Mellons RDC v Newport Corporation* (1950)).

5. This statement was criticised by Lord Simonds in the same case on appeal to the House of Lords, when he said that it was 'a naked usurpation of the legislative function under the thin guise of interpretation'.

6. The decision in *Pepper v Hart* (1993) on the use of *Hansard* showed a move towards a more activist role although there are limitations on its use.

7. It is yet to be seen whether the Supreme Court will be more activist than the former House of Lords.

8. However, the courts in general appear to be using a more activist approach, eg in *R(Ghai) v Newcastle upon Tyne City Council* (2010), where the Court of Appeal took a 'generous' rather than 'restricted' meaning of the word 'building' in the Cremation Act 1902.

4

European Union law

THE INSTITUTIONS

Council – government representatives

Commission – 27 independent commissioners

Parliament – 785 directly elected MEPs

↕

EUROPEAN UNION

↓

SOURCES OF LAW

Treaties – directly applicable

Regulations – directly applicable

Directives – vertical direct effect

↓

EFFECT ON SOVEREIGNTY

EU law takes priority over national law

Van Gend en Loos (1963)

Factortame (1990)

The European Union (originally the European Economic Community) was founded in 1957 with six members. The United Kingdom joined in 1973 and by 1995 Union membership increased to 15. Another ten countries joined on 1 May 2004 and two more countries in 2007, making a total of 27 Member States.

The founding treaty was the Treaty of Rome 1957. This has now been replaced with two treaties: the Treaty on European Union (TEU) and the Treaty on the Functioning of the European Union (TFEU).

4.1 The institutions

4.1.1 The Council of the European Union

1. The Council is attended by a government representative of each Member State who must be 'at ministerial level, authorised to commit the government of that Member State' (Article 16 TEU).
2. The Presidency is held by each Member State in rotation for a period of six months.
3. The Council is the principal decision-making body of the Union.
4. Sensitive areas such as taxation and social security must be decided by a unanimous vote.
5. For most other matters decisions are made by a qualified majority on a weighted voting basis. Each state has a set number of votes based on its population size.

4.1.2 The Commission

1. There are 27 Commissioners who are appointed for a five-year term, one from each Member State.
2. Commissioners must act in the best interests of the Union. They must 'refrain from any activity incompatible with their duties' (Article 245 TFEU).
3. The Commission is the motivating force behind Union policy. It proposes policies and presents drafts of legislation to the Council for consideration by the Council.
4. The Commission is also the 'guardian of the treaties' and ensures that treaty provisions and other measures are implemented by Member States.

5. The Commission may refer an infringement by a Member State to the European Court of Justice (Article 258 TFEU).

6. It also has investigative powers over alleged infringements (Article 245 TFEU).

7. It is responsible for the administration of the Union and has executive powers to implement the Union's budget.

4.1.3 The Parliament

1. Members of the Parliament are elected by the citizens of the Member States. Elections take place once every five years. There are 78 MEPs from the UK.

2. The Parliament has no direct law-making authority. Its role is to discuss proposals and put questions to the Council and the Commission.

3. However, it has some important control functions. It has power to dismiss the Commission by passing a vote of censure (Article 234 TFEU). In 1999 the entire Commission resigned to forestall such a censure vote.

4. The Parliament has some power over the budget, especially on non-necessary expenditure.

5. Under Article 228 TFEU, the Parliament may appoint an Ombudsman to receive complaints of maladminstration by the Union institutions. The first Ombudsman was appointed in 1995.

4.1.4 Other representative bodies

1. The Economic and Social Committee advises the Commission and the Council on economic matters.

2. It consists of 'representatives of organisations of employers, of the employed, and of other parties' representative of civil society, notably in socio-economic, civic, professional and cultural areas' (Article 300 TFEU).

3. The Committee of the Regions advises the Commission and the Council on regional matters.

4.1.5 The European Court of Justice

1. The function of the court is 'to ensure that in the interpretation and application of the Treaty the law is observed' (Article 19 TEU).

2. There are 27 judges (one from each Member State) who are appointed from those eligible for appointment to the highest judicial posts in their own country (Article 252 TFEU).

3. The court is assisted by eight Advocates-General whose task is to research all the legal points involved and 'to present publicly, with complete impartiality and independence, reasoned conclusions on cases submitted to the Court of Justice with a view to assisting the latter in the performance of its duties' (Article 253 TFEU).

4. The court has wide jurisdiction over Union law. It hears cases brought by the institutions, Member States or individuals alleging a breach of Union law. A main area here is the role of the Commission in bringing cases against Member States.

5. It also hears cases referred by courts in any Member State for a preliminary ruling on a point of Union law (Article 267 TFEU).

6. Such referrals are mandatory where no further appeal is possible in the Member State's court system and discretionary from any other court.

7. The European Court of Justice operates in a different way to English courts. The main differences are:
   - cases are presented on paper with only limited oral argument;
   - an Advocate-General is used to present an independent view of the law;
   - judgments are always given in a written form as the decision of the whole court; it is never revealed if there were any dissenting judges;
   - the court is not bound by its own previous decisions;
   - the court uses the purposive approach to interpretation.

4.2 Sources of law

Source	Effect	Cases
Treaties	Directly applicable	*van Duyn* (1974
	Have both vertical and horizontal direct effect	*Macarthys v Smith* (1980)
Regulations Art 288 TFEU	Directly applicable	*Re Tachographs* (1979)
	Have both vertical and horizontal direct effect	*Leonesio* (1972)
Directives Art 288 TFEU	Have vertical direct effect	*Marshall* (1986)
	Do *not* have horizontal direct effect	*Duke v GEC* (1988)
	Can sue State under *Francovich* principle	*Francovich* (1991)
Recommendations and opinions Art 288 TFEU	'Soft' law	
	Must be taken into consideration when interpreting law	*Grimaldi* (1989)

Effect of the different sources of law

4.2.1 Treaties

1. Treaties are the primary source of European Union law.
2. All Treaties are 'without further enactment to be given legal effect or used in the United Kingdom' (s2(1) European Communities Act 1972).
3. Treaties are therefore directly applicable and, where a Treaty creates individual rights, then those rights can be relied on by an individual (*Van Duyn v Home Office* (1974), *Macarthys Ltd v Smith* (1980)).

4.2.2 Regulations

1. Regulations are issued under Article 288 TFEU.

2. This makes the effect of Regulations 'binding in every respect and directly applicable in each Member State'.

3. Member States must enforce Regulations; they have no choice over whether to bring them into effect (*Commission v UK: Re Tachographs* (1979)).

4. Regulations have vertical and horizontal direct effect. This means that citizens may rely on them both against the State and against other private individuals or bodies (*Leonesio v Ministero dell'Agricoltura* (1972)).

4.2.3 Directives

1. Directives are issued under Article 288 TFEU.

2. Directives 'bind any Member State to which they are addressed as to the result to be achieved, while leaving to domestic agencies a competence as to form and means'.

3. They are issued with a time limit for implementation in the Member States. If a Directive is not implemented it will have vertical direct effect when the time limit for implementation expires. So where the Directive creates individual rights, those rights may be relied on against the State or an 'arm of the State' (*Marshall v Southampton and South West Hampshire Area Health Authority* (1986)).

4. The concept of an 'arm of the State' is a body that has been made responsible for providing a public service under the control of the State (*Foster v British Gas plc* (1990)).

5. However, Directives that have not been implemented do not have horizontal direct effect. They cannot be relied on against private individuals or bodies (*Duke v GEC Reliance Ltd* (1988), *Dori v Recreb Srl* (1994)).

6. Where a Directive has not been implemented, an individual who suffers loss as a result of the non-implementation may sue the State for their breach of Community law (*Francovich v Italian Republic* (1991)).

7. In *Dori v Recreb Srl* (1994) the European Court of Justice held that compensation would be payable where:
   - the purpose of the Directive was to grant rights to individuals;
   - those rights could be identified from the Directive;
   - there was a causal link between the breach of the State's obligations and the damage suffered.

8. In *R v HM Treasury, ex parte British Telecommunications plc* (1996) the court said that compensation would be payable only where the breach was sufficiently serious.

4.2.4 Recommendations and Opinions

1. These are also issued under Article 288 TFEU. Neither creates enforceable rights.

2. However, national courts are bound to take them into consideration when interpreting national law adopted to give effect to a Recommendation (*Grimaldi v Fondes des Maladies Professionelles* (1989)).

3. This effect is known as 'soft law', as opposed to the 'hard law' effect of legislation with binding force.

4.3 Effect on sovereignty of Parliament

4.3.1 Conflict between EU law and national law

1. In *Van Gend en Loos* (1963), where there was a conflict between the Treaty of Rome and an earlier Dutch law, the European Court of Justice said that 'the Member States have limited their sovereign rights, albeit within limited fields, and have created a body of law which binds both their nationals and themselves'.

2. In *Costa v ENEL* (1964) there was a conflict between a number of Treaty provisions and a later Italian law, which under Italian law would take priority. The European Court of Justice held that 'The reception, within the laws of each Member State, of provisions having a Community source . . . has as a corollary the impossibility, for the Member State, to give preference to a unilateral and subsequent measure . . .'.

3. In *Internationale Handelsgesellschaft mbH* (1970) the court held that an EU regulation that conflicted with the German constitution took precedence over the German law.

4. In *Simmenthal SpA (No 2)* (1979) the court stated that national courts are under a duty to give full effect to the provisions of EU law and, if necessary, should refuse to apply national laws that conflict with EU law.

4.3.2 Sovereignty of Parliament

1. The fact that EU takes precedence over national law means that while the UK is a member of the Union, Parliament is no longer the supreme law-maker.

2. This was stressed when the validity of the Merchant Shipping Act 1988 was successfully challenged as it conflicted with the Treaty of Rome (*R v Secretary of State for Transport, ex parte Factortame* (1990)).

3. Domestic courts are under a duty to apply EU law in preference to national law.

5

Law reform

Need for law reform

- Law made piecemeal
- Many obsolete statutes
- Low priority for Parliament
- Judges limited in powers to reform

LAW REFORM

Law Commission

- Established by Law Commission Act 1965
- Full-time
- Five commissioners
- Researches/consults
- Report + draft Bill
- Many reforms
- Failure to codify
- 70% of reports enacted

Other law reform bodies

- Law Reform Committee
- Criminal Law Revision Committee
- Royal Commissions, eg Phillip Commission
- Various *ad hoc* committees and reviews, eg Woolf Review

5.1 The need for law reform

1. English law has developed in a piecemeal fashion; there is no code of law, unlike in many European countries.

2. Judges can only reform law on individual points that come before the courts as cases arise (eg *R v R* (1991), making marital rape an offence).

3. Parliament has many other functions, and reform of 'lawyers' law' in particular often takes a low priority (eg the failure to implement the Draft Code of Criminal Law).

4. There are many statutes that have become obsolete, but which have never been repealed.

5. Before 1965 there were only part-time law reform bodies, such as the Law Reform Committee and the Criminal Law Revision Committee.

6. It was felt that there was a need for a full-time law reform body, so the Law Commission was created.

5.2 Law Commission

5.2.1 Composition and working

1. This was established by the Law Commissions Act 1965.

2. It is a full-time body with a chairman, who is a High Court Judge seconded to the Law Commission for a term of three years, and four other Law Commissioners.

3. Its role is:
   - to systematically develop and reform the law;
   - to simplify and modernise the law;
   - to codify the law;
   - to eliminate anomalies;
   - to repeal obsolete and unnecessary enactments.

4. The Lord Chancellor may refer topics to the Law Commission, but most topics are selected by the Commission itself, which then seeks governmental approval to draft a report on the topic.

5. The area of law is researched, then a consultation paper is published setting out the current law, the problems with it and possible options for reform.

6. After consultation, the Commission will draw up positive proposals for reform. These will be presented in a report which will also set out the research that led to the conclusions.

7. A draft Bill may be attached to the report showing precisely how the law should be reformed.

5.2.2 Implementation of reports

1. Overall about 70% of the Law Commission's reports have eventually led to legislation.

2. However, the rate has not been consistent. In the first ten years 85% of reports were enacted by Parliament. In the next ten years only 50% became law. In 1990 not one proposal was made law.

3. In the early 1990s a Special Standing Committee of the House of Lords considered Law Commission draft Bills and this led to an increase in the number of reports which were implemented.

4. The lack of parliamentary commitment to law reform has been frequently commented on by successive chairmen of the Law Commission in their annual reports.

5. A major area that has been ignored by Parliament is the reform of the criminal law. In 1985 a Draft Criminal Code was published by the Law Commission. No part of this was ever implemented by Parliament.

6. In 2008 the Law Commission stated that it would be concentrating on smaller areas of the code, as there was more chance that the Government would be prepared to make such reforms of the law.

7. In the last ten years the Government has implemented many Law Commission reports.

5.2.3 Achievements of the Law Commission

1. Many Acts of Parliament have been enacted as the result of Law Commission reports.

2. Examples include:
   - Occupiers' Liability Act 1984;
   - Law Reform (Year and a Day Rule) Act 1996;
   - Contract (Rights of Third Parties) Act 1999;
   - Land Registration Act 2002;

- Fraud Act 2006;
- Corporate Manslaughter and Corporate Homicide Act 2007.

3. The Law Commission has also 'tidied up' the statute book with the repeal of over 2,000 obsolete statutes.

5.3 Other law reform bodies

1. The part-time Law Reform Committee still contributes to law reform of civil law (eg Latent Damage Act 1986) and is consulted by the Law Commission on certain areas, eg trust law.

2. The part-time Criminal Law Revision Committee sat from 1957 to 1987 and one of its main achievements was the reform of the law of theft and related offences in the Theft Act 1968.

3. Temporary commissions or committees are used to review one specific area of law or the legal system. These are often chaired by a judge, with the commission being referred to by the name of that judge. Some of their proposals may become law. Examples include:
   - the Royal Commission on Police Procedure (Phillips Commission 1981), which led to the Police and Criminal Evidence Act 1984;
   - the Royal Commission on Criminal Justice (Runciman Commission 1993), some of whose recommendations were implemented in the Criminal Appeal Act 1995 and the Criminal Procedure and Investigations Act 1996;
   - the Woolf Review of the civil justice system, which led to the Civil Procedure Rules 1999 and wide-ranging reform of the system.

4. Judges and business people are increasingly being asked to review areas of the legal system and the law, eg the Auld Review (2001) on the criminal justice system, David Clementi's review on the provision of legal services (2004) and Lord Carter's review of legal funding in 2006.

6

The civil justice system

PROBLEMS
- Expensive
- Delays
- Complex
- Adversarial
- Inefficient

WOOLF REFORMS
- Three-track system
- Encourage ADR
- Time limits
- Judicial case management

BY THE COURTS

DISPUTE RESOLUTION

BY ADR

Negotiation
- Parties themselves
- Informal
- Cheapest
- Quickest

Mediation/Conciliation
- Third party facilitates
- Cheap
- Quick

Arbitration
- More formal
- Expensive
- Binding (Arbitration Act 1996)

Civil justice has always been seen as too expensive and too complex, with long delays. In 1999 the Woolf reforms of the civil justice system tried to address these problems.

6.1 The court structure

6.1.1 The three tracks

All cases that are defended are allocated to one of three tracks.

1. Small claims track – this is for most cases under £5,000. Note that the normal limit for housing disrepair cases and personal injury cases is £1,000, while illegal eviction and harassment cases are excluded from the small claims track.

2. Fast track cases – these are claims for between £5,000 and £25,000, although cases of this amount involving a complex point of law can be allocated to the multi-track.

3. Multi-track cases – these are claims over £25,000, or complex cases for less than this amount.

6.1.2 The civil courts

1. There are two civil courts that hear cases at first instance. These are the County Court and the High Court.

2. The County Court hears all small claims cases and all fast track cases. County Courts, which are designated as Civil Trial Centres, can also deal with multi-track cases above £25,000. However, unless the parties agree, cases above £50,000 in value are not usually tried in the County Court.

3. The High Court has three divisions.
   - Queen's Bench Division – for contract and tort claims; there are also special courts in the Commercial List, Technology and Construction List, and in the Admiralty Court.
   - Chancery Division – for disputes involving matters such as mortgages, trusts, copyright and patents; winding up of companies is dealt with by the Companies Court within this Division.
   - Family Division – for family-related disputes, wardship cases and cases relating to children under the Children Act 1989.

4. In 2005 the Government started consulting on the possibility of combining the civil courts into one court.

6.2 Procedure in outline

1. The Civil Procedure Rules 1999 set out the rules for each stage of a case.

2. The overriding objective of the Rules is to enable the court to deal with cases justly, by:
    - ensuring that the parties in any case are on an equal footing;
    - dealing with cases in a way which is proportionate to the amount involved and the importance of the case.

3. Parties are encouraged to disclose the facts of their case prior to starting any court case. For some types of claim (eg personal injury) a pre-action protocol must be followed.

4. All claims for less than £25,000 must be started in the County Court. Claims for more than this amount can be started in either the High Court or the County Court, except personal injury claims for less than £50,000, which must be started in the County Court.

5. Most types of claim are started by issuing a Part 7 claim form. Particulars of a claim must be included on the claim form, or attached to it, or served separately within 14 days of the claim form being served.

6. There must also be a statement of truth as to the facts in the particulars of the claim.

7. The claim form and the particulars of the claim must be served on the defendant. This may be done by the court or the claimant and can be served personally, by post, by fax, by e-mail or other electronic means.

8. The defendant has 14 days in which to respond. A defendant may:
    - pay the claim;
    - admit or partly admit it;
    - file an acknowledgement of service (but then must file a defence within another 14 days);
    - file a defence.

9. A defence that just denies the claim is not sufficient; it should be more specific.

10. At any point before or after the commencement of proceedings, the defendant or the claimant may make a Part 36 offer (to settle) and payment.

6.2.1 Allocation of cases

1. When a defence is filed at court, an allocation questionnaire is sent to all parties. This helps the judge decide which track the case should be allocated to.

2. An allocation fee has to be paid at this stage, but not for claims under £1,500.

3. If a party is dissatisfied with the allocation decision, an application can be made to the court for the claim to be re-allocated.

6.2.2 Small claims procedure

1. Cases are heard by a District Judge who will normally use an interventionist approach.

2. Cases are dealt with in a relatively informal way, although they are now heard in open court. Prior to the 1999 reforms small claims cases were heard in private.

3. The use of lawyers is discouraged because the winning party cannot recover the costs of using a lawyer from the losing side.

4. There may be a paper adjudication if the judge thinks it is appropriate and the parties agree.

6.2.3 Fast track cases

1. The concept of the fast track was described by Lord Woolf as 'intended to provide improved access to justice . . . by providing a strictly limited procedure designed to take cases to trial in a short but reasonable time-scale at a fixed cost'.

2. There are standard directions by the court for trial preparation.

3. There should be a maximum delay of 30 weeks between directions and trial.

4. Normally only one expert witness is allowed and, if the parties cannot agree on an expert, the court has power to appoint one. The expert's evidence will be given in writing.

5. There are fixed costs for the advocate at the trial.

6.2.4 Multi-track cases

1. There is no standard procedure for pre-trial directions; the judge has flexibility to use a number of different approaches, including case management conferences and pre-trial reviews.

2. The aim is to identify the issues as early as possible and, where appropriate, try specific issues prior to the main trial. This is aimed at encouraging a settlement.

3. The number of expert witnesses is controlled by the court as the court's permission is needed for any party to use an expert to give evidence (oral or written).

4. All time limits are strictly enforced. An approximate date for the trial (a 'trial window') is given to the parties and the court is very unlikely to agree to any adjournment.

6.3 Appeals

6.3.1 Appeal routes

Court of Appeal (Civil Division)

Circuit Judge → High Court Judge

case heard by District Judge

case heard by Circuit Judge

Appeals in small claims and fast track cases

1. Since 2000 appeals may be made in small claims cases under Rule 52 CPR; the route is for an appeal from a decision by a District Judge to go to a Circuit Judge. Appeals for small claims were introduced in order to comply with the European Convention on Human Rights.

2. Appeals for fast track cases depend on which level of judge heard the case. An appeal from a District Judge goes to a Circuit Judge; an appeal from a Circuit Judge goes to a High Court Judge.

3. A second appeal to the Court of Appeal (Civil Division) may only be made where the Court of Appeal considers that:
   a) the appeal would raise an important point of principle or practice; or
   b) there is some other compelling reason for the Court of Appeal to hear it (s55(1) Access to Justice Act 1999).

This has the effect that second appeals for small claims or fast track cases will become a rarity (*Tanfern Ltd v Cameron-Macdonald* (2000)).

Supreme Court

↑

Court of Appeal (Civil Division)

↑

All appeals from High Court

and

County Court multi-track cases

Appeals in multi-track cases

4. Appeals from the final decision in a multi-track case heard in the County Court go to the Court of Appeal.

5. All appeals from decisions of the High Court go to the Court of Appeal. The exception to this is where an appeal is made direct to the Supreme Court under the leapfrog procedure (Administration of Justice Act 1969).

6. In a multi-track case where there has been an appeal to the Court of Appeal, then a further appeal to the Supreme Court is possible.

6.3.2 The approach to appeals

1. Permission to appeal is usually required; this can be from either the trial court or the relevant appeal court.

2. Permission will only be granted where the court considers that:
   - an appeal would have a real prospect of success; or
   - there is some other compelling reason why the appeal should be heard.

3. The prospect of success must be realistic rather than fanciful (*Swain v Hillman* (1999)).

4. Permission to appeal is not required where the liberty of the individual is in issue, eg an appeal against a committal order.

5. Rule 52.11 states that an appeal will only be allowed (ie successful) where the decision of the lower court was wrong or where it was unjust because of a serious procedural or other irregularity.

6.4 Comment on the post-Woolf civil system

1. It is generally felt that the reforms are a qualified success.

2. The adversarial approach has been replaced by more co-operation between parties, and the use of ADR has increased.

3. The real issues of cases are being defined more quickly and this is leading to more cases settling and earlier settlements (rather than 'court door' settlements on the day of the trial).

4. The main problems are that:
   - the system is heavily front loaded, both in work to be done and in cost;
   - the new procedures, such as pre-action protocols, allocation questionnaires and case management conferences, are more complex;
   - the rules on time limits are very strictly enforced, eg *Vinos v Marks and Spencer plc* (2000), where the claim was struck out because the claim form was served nine days after the expiry of the time.

5. There is a less adversarial culture and a greater willingness to 'put cards on the table', with insurance companies more prepared to settle.

6. The main disadvantages include:
   - in PI cases front loading of work means that costs have gone up;
   - delay is not improved as solicitors do more work before opening negotiations.

6.5 Alternative dispute resolution

6.5.1 Negotiation

1. This is an informal approach between the parties themselves or their lawyers.
2. It is completely private and is the quickest and cheapest method of resolving a dispute.

6.5.2 Mediation/conciliation

1. Mediation is a process in which a neutral person (the mediator) helps the parties reach a compromise solution to their dispute. The mediator will discuss the position of each party with them and what outcomes they want from the dispute, but will not usually offer an opinion. The emphasis is on the parties themselves working out a solution.
2. Conciliation goes beyond mediation in that the mediator (or conciliator) has power to suggest grounds for compromise and the possible basis for a settlement.
3. There are a number of mediation/conciliation services, eg the Centre for Dispute Resolution.
4. ADR allows the parties to have control over the resolution process as they can withdraw at any time and a solution cannot be imposed on them – they must agree to it.
5. The process is preferred to court proceedings as it is:
   - cheaper;
   - quicker;
   - more informal;
   - conducive to business relations remaining more amicable between the parties.
6. The main disadvantage is that neither mediation or conciliation will necessarily lead to an agreement.

6.5.3 Arbitration

1. This is the voluntary submission by the parties of their dispute to the judgment of an arbitrator (or panel of arbitrators) who is neutral.

2. The agreement to arbitrate is usually in writing, and written arbitration agreements are governed by the Arbitration Act 1996.

3. The agreement to go to arbitration can be made before a dispute arises (usually by a *Scott v Avery* clause in a contract) or after the dispute has arisen.

4. The agreement will either name an arbitrator or provide a method of choosing one. If the parties cannot agree on an arbitrator the court can be asked to appoint one (Arbitration Act 1996).

5. The procedure for the arbitration hearing agreed by the parties can range from a 'paper' arbitration to a very formal court-like procedure.

6. The decision by the arbitrator is called an award. It is binding on the parties and can be enforced through the courts if necessary.

7. An award by an arbitrator can only be challenged in the courts on the grounds of serious irregularity in the proceedings or on a point of law (ss68, 69 Arbitration Act 1996).

8. The main advantages of arbitration are:
   - expertise – where the arbitrator has specialist knowledge;
   - flexibility – ability to choose time, place and type of procedure;
   - privacy – the facts of the dispute are not made public;
   - speed – although commercial and international arbitrations are subject to delays;
   - cost – although the use of specialist arbitrators can be expensive.

9. The main disadvantage is that legal points are not suitable for decision by a non-lawyer.

7

Tribunals and Inquiries

Administrative

- Created by statute
- Enforcement of social and welfare rights, e.g.
  a) social security
  b) employment
  c) immigration etc.
- Usually panel of three
- More informal and cheaper than court

Domestic tribunals

- Internal disciplinary
- Some created by statute, eg Solicitors Disciplinary Tribunal
- Some have right of appeal to Privy Council

TRIBUNALS

Control of tribunals

1 Administrative Justice and Tribunals Council
- created by the Tribunals, Courts and Enforcement Act 2007
- keeps system under review
- makes proposals for change
2 The Courts
- judicial review
- three prerogative orders
  a) mandatory order
  b) prohibitory order
  c) quashing irder

Inquiries

- Set up to investigate a specific issue
- May be set up under a statutory power
- Fact-finding exercise
- Work of statutory inquiries is reviewed by the Administrative Justice and Tribunals Council

7.1 Administrative tribunals

A system of tribunals operates alongside the court system. Each type of tribunal specialises in a certain type of case. Cases concerning these particular matters must go to the appropriate tribunal and not to a court.

7.1.1 History of tribunals

1. During the second half of the twentieth century, different tribunals were set up to deal with people's rights in a variety of administrative areas such as benefits for disability, rent, education, employment and immigration.

2. There were over 70 different tribunals operating in about 2,000 panels around the country.

3. There was no uniformity. Each tribunal developed its own rules.

4. There was no consistent appeal route. For some tribunals there was no appeal route. Other tribunals had a special appeal tribunal, such as the Employment Appeal Tribunal.

5. This unsatisfactory system was criticised in the Leggat Report (2001).

7.1.2 The unified tribunal system

1. Following the Leggatt Report, the Tribunals, Courts and Enforcement Act 2007 set up a new tribunal system.

2. There is a First Tier Tribunal to hear cases at first instance.

3. The First Tier Tribunal sits in seven chambers, each chamber specialising in certain types of case, such as social entitlement, health, education and social care cases, asylum and immigration cases or taxation cases.

4. The appeal route from the First Tier Tribunal is to the Upper Tribunal.

5. From the Upper Tribunal there is a further possible appeal route to the Court of Appeal and from here to the Supreme Court.

6. Note that employment tribunals are not yet included in the new unified system. They remain separate and have their own appeal route.

7.1.3 Composition and Procedure

1. The proceedings are heard by a tribunal judge. The selection of tribunal judges is carried out by the Judicial Appointments Commission.

2. For some topics two lay members will sit with the judge to make the decision. These lay members will have expertise in the particular field of the tribunal.

3. There are rules for the procedure in the various chambers. These have common elements and are aimed at creating a harmonised system of rules.

4. Alternative dispute resolution is encouraged and pilot schemes are being used to see how different forms of ADR might be used instead of using the relevant tribunal.

7.1.4 Advantages and disadvantages of tribunals

1. Advantages are:
   - speed – cases are usually dealt with more quickly than in the courts;
   - cost-effectiveness – taking a case to a tribunal is much cheaper than court proceedings as there are no fees and costs are not normally awarded;
   - expertise – each tribunal chamber operates in a specialised field and often has lay members with specialist knowledge;
   - informality – documentation is kept simple.

2. The disadvantages are:
   - some areas, eg social security, have very complex regulations that the applicant may not understand;
   - government funding to help an individual with a case is not available for most tribunals cases (except Mental Health Review cases and Immigration cases);
   - the individual will usually be claiming against a government department or a business, which are more likely to be represented by lawyers – this creates an imbalance between the parties.

7.2 Control of tribunals

7.2.1 Administrative Justice and Tribunals Council

1. The Tribunals, Courts and Enforcement Act 2007 set up the Administrative Justice and Tribunals Council (AJTC).

2. This replaced the Council on Tribunals.

3. The AJTC has wider powers than the Council on Tribunals. Its duties include:
   (a) keeping the working of tribunals under review;
   (b) reporting on the constitution and working of tribunals;
   (c) considering and reporting on any other matter relating to tribunals.

4. A member of the Council may attend (as observer) any proceedings of a tribunal.

7.2.2 Control by the courts

1. The main control is by judicial review. Any party to a tribunal hearing who believes that the rules of natural justice have been breached can apply to the Queen's Bench Divisional Court for the decision to be reviewed.

2. The main rules of natural justice are that:
   - there is a duty to hear both sides before a decision is made (*Baldwin v Ridge* (1964));
   - no one should be a judge in his own cause (*R v Altrincham Justices, ex parte Pennington* (1975)).

3. Since the Human Rights Act 1998 came into effect the test for whether there is perceived bias (as opposed to actual bias) in a case is an objective one. Would the fair-minded observer consider there was a real danger of bias? (*Director General of Fair Trading v The Proprietary Association of Great Britain* (2001)).

4. The court has three 'prerogative' orders it may make when there has been a breach of natural justice. These are:
   - a mandatory order, which orders the inferior court or tribunal to perform a duty, eg to hear a case;
   - a prohibitory order, which prevents it from hearing a case that it has no power to deal with;
   - a quashing order, which removes the decision to the High Court so that its legality can be enquired into and, if it is found to be invalid, the decision quashed.

7.3 Domestic tribunals

1. These are internal private disciplinary bodies that operate in different institutions, such as the professions, trade unions and universities.

2. Most have been set up by the particular institution, although some have been established by statute, such as the Solicitors Disciplinary Tribunal under the Solicitors Act 1974.

3. Where the tribunal was established by statute, there will usually be an appeal route from its decisions. For example, an appeal from the decision by the General Medical Council to strike off a doctor can be made to the Judicial Committee of the Privy Council.

4. All are subject to the laws of natural justice and their decisions may be judicially reviewed.

7.4 Inquiries

1. Inquiries are set up as and when necessary to investigate a specific issue.

2. Some inquiries may be set up under a statutory power, eg under s49 of the Police Act 1996 the Home Secretary can do so for any matter connected to policing in an area. This power was used to set up the Macpherson Inquiry in the Stephen Lawrence case (1997–98).

3. Even if there is no statutory power, Parliament may resolve to set up an inquiry into any matter of public importance. Often a judge will be appointed to head such an inquiry, eg the Scott Inquiry into the sale of arms to Iraq (1996) and the inquiry by Dame Janet Smith into the Shipman murders (2004).

4. Inquiries will sit in public unless this is against the public interest. They have the power to call witnesses and order the production of relevant documents or other evidence.

5. They are a fact-finding exercise and will issue a report on the matter; they cannot make any decision on any of the issues. Their findings may, however, be used as the basis for reforming the law.

6. Inquiries are subject to judicial review. They cannot go beyond their remit, as shown in *R v Chairman of Stephen Lawrence Inquiry, ex parte A* (1998), where the inquiry could not put certain questions to witnesses as its task was to examine the conduct of the police investigation into the murder of Stephen Lawrence and not to conduct a trial of the people suspected of the murder.

7. The work of statutory inquiries is reviewed by the Administrative Justice and Tribunals Council.

8

Police powers

	POLICE POWERS	
Power	**Statutory provision**	**Comment**
Stop and search	• ss1–7 PACE • also under other Acts, eg Misuse of Drugs Act 1971	• only in place to which the public have access • must have reasonable grounds for suspecting stolen or prohibited goods
Search of premises	• by search warrant (s8 PACE) • to arrest someone (s17 PACE) • after arrest (ss 18 and 32 PACE) • breach of the peace	• magistrates issue warrant • warrant must be shown before search
Arrest	• with a warrant • a constable can arrest for any offence but must have reasonable grounds for believing that it is necessary (s24 PACE)	• magistrates issue warrant • warrant must be shown as soon as practicable after arrest
Detention	• ss34–36 PACE • 24 hours normal limit • for indictable offences this can be extended to 96 hours with magistrates' permission	Detainee has right to: • have someone informed • have legal advice • see a copy of the Codes of Practice
Interviews	• s53 PACE • ss34–39 Criminal Justice and Public Order Act 1994 places limits on right to silence	• must be tape-recorded • those under 17 or vulnerable must have an appropriate adult present

8.1 Stop and search

8.1.1 Powers to stop and search

1. A police constable may stop and search people and vehicles in a place to which the public has access (s1 PACE 1984).

2. A place to which the public has access includes a place where they have paid for entry; it also includes a garden or yard of a private property where the constable has reasonable grounds for believing that the person does not reside there and has not got the permission of the resident to be there.

3. In order to stop a vehicle the constable must be in uniform (s2(9)(b) PACE).

4. In order to search a person or vehicle the constable must have reasonable grounds for suspecting that he will find stolen or prohibited articles (s1(3) PACE).

5. Police officers also have specific powers to stop and search under other legislation such as the Misuse of Drugs Act 1971 and the anti-terrorism legislation.

8.1.2 Safeguards on the power to stop and search

1. If a constable is not in uniform then he must produce documentary evidence that he is a police officer.

2. In all cases, before commencing the search the constable must state his name and station to the suspect, specify the object of the proposed search and the grounds for proposing the search.

3. If this is not done then the search is unlawful (*Osman v DPP* (1999)).

4. If the search is in public, the constable can only request the removal of an outer coat, jacket and gloves (s2(9)(a) PACE).

5. Code of Practice A gives the police guidance on the use of the stop and search powers. In particular it points out that reasonable suspicion can never be supported on the basis of personal factors alone. Factors such as age, colour, hairstyle, manner of dress or a known previous conviction cannot be used as the sole basis on which to search.

8.2 Searching premises

8.2.1 Search warrants

1. A search warrant can be issued by a magistrate allowing police to search premises.

2. Under s8 PACE, such a warrant will only be issued where there are reasonable grounds for believing that:
   - an indictable offence has been committed; and
   - there is material on the premises which is likely to be of substantial value to the investigation of the offence; and
   - the material is likely to be relevant evidence; and
   - it is not practicable to communicate with any person entitled to grant entry to the premises or the material; or
   - entry to the premises will not be granted unless a warrant is granted; or
   - the purpose of the search may be frustrated or seriously prejudiced unless a constable arriving at the premises can gain immediate entry.

3. Search warrants can also be granted under other Acts. These include powers to search for stolen goods, drugs or firearms.

4. A warrant can be a 'specific premises' warrant to search a named address or it can be an 'all premises' warrant which allows all premises occupied or controlled by the defendant to be searched.

5. A search warrant can provide for access on more than one occasion.

8.2.2 Other powers to enter premises

1. Police may enter without a search warrant to arrest a person (on a warrant), or for an indictable offence, or to recapture an escaped prisoner (s17 PACE).

2. If a person is arrested, the police can enter and search premises that were occupied or controlled by him (s18 PACE).

3. If a person is arrested, the police can enter and search premises in which he was at the time of arrest or immediately before the arrest (s32 PACE).

4. There is a common law right to enter premises in order to prevent or deal with a breach of the peace. This right exists even though the

breach of the peace is in private property (*McLeod v Commissioner of Police of the Metropolis* (1994)).

5. The police may enter and search any premises where the occupier consents to this.

8.2.3 Safeguards on police powers to search premises

1. Where a warrant has been issued the police are required to enter and search at a reasonable hour, unless the purpose of the search might be frustrated (s16(4) PACE and Code of Practice B para 5).

2. The police must identify themselves to the occupier of any premises searched: they must show the search warrant to him and give him a copy (s16(5) PACE). However, this need not be done on entry, but must be done before any search commences (*R v Longman* (1988)).

3. Where the entry is under s17 or s18, the police must give anyone present in the premises the reason for the entry. If they do not do so the entry is unlawful (*O'Loughlin v Chief Constable of Essex* (1998)).

4. The police can only exercise powers to enter and search under s32 immediately after arrest (*R v Badham* (1987)).

8.3 Powers of arrest

8.3.1 Powers of arrest

1. The Serious Organised Crime and Police Act 2005 amended s24 of PACE so that the category of arrestable offence is abandoned. Instead, a constable can make an arrest for any offence.

   ■ Section 24(1) of PACE states that a constable may arrest without a warrant:
   (a) anyone who is about to commit an offence;
   (b) anyone who is in the act of committing an offence;
   (c) anyone whom he has reasonable grounds for suspecting to be about to commit an offence;
   (d) anyone whom he has reasonable grounds for suspecting to be committing an offence.

   ■ Section 24(2) of PACE states that if a constable has reasonable grounds for suspecting that an offence has been committed, he may arrest without a warrant anyone whom he has reasonable grounds to suspect of being guilty of it.

- Section 24(3) of PACE states that if an offence has been committed, a constable may arrest without a warrant:
  - (a) anyone who is guilty of the offence; or
  - (b) anyone whom he has reasonable grounds for suspecting to be guilty of it.

2. However, a constable can only arrest if he has reasonable grounds for believing that it is necessary to make the arrest for one of the following reasons:
   - to enable the person's name or address to be ascertained;
   - to prevent the person from:
     - causing physical injury to himself or any other person;
     - suffering physical injury;
     - causing loss of or damage to property;
     - committing an offence against public decency;
     - causing an unlawful obstruction of the highway;
   - to protect a child or other vulnerable person;
   - to allow the prompt and effective investigation of the offence or of the conduct of the person;
   - to prevent any prosecution for the offence from being hindered by the disappearance of the person in question.

3. Code of Practice G gives guidelines on making arrests. It points out that a lawful arrest requires two elements:
   - (a) a person's involvement or suspected involvement or attempted involvement; and
   - (b) reasonable grounds for believing that the person's arrest is necessary.

4. Code G also points out that arresting officers are required to inform the person arrested that they have been arrested, even if this fact is obvious, and of the relevant circumstances in respect to both elements.

8.3.2 Arrests with a warrant

1. An application for a warrant for arrest may be made under s1 Magistrates' Court Act 1980.

2. The application must be supported by written information and also by sworn oral evidence showing that the person has committed or is suspected of committing an offence punishable by imprisonment.

3. A warrant must name the person to be arrested.

8.3.3 Other powers of arrest

1. There are some additional statutory powers to make an arrest, eg where a person granted police bail has failed to attend the police station on the set date (s46A PACE).

2. There is still a common law power to arrest for breach of the peace.

8.3.4 Procedure on arrest

1. It must be made clear to the person that they are being arrested and what the arrest is for.

2. Where necessary reasonable force may used to effect the arrest (s117 PACE).

3. If the arrest is made by a warrant, then that warrant must be shown on demand as soon as is reasonably practicable.

4. The police may search the arrested person for anything which might be used to make an escape or for evidence relating to the offence.

5. If the search takes place in public, the police can only require the suspect to remove outer coat, jacket and gloves.

6. If the arrest is not made at a police station, the suspect must be taken to a police station as soon as practicable (s30(1) PACE).

7. However, there may be a delay if it is necessary to carry out certain investigations immediately and the presence of the suspect is necessary in order to carry out those investigations (s30(10) PACE).

8. If there is a delay in taking a suspect to a police station the reasons for the delay must be recorded on arrival at the police station (s30(11) PACE).

8.4 Detention at the police station

8.4.1 Time limits and the custody officer's role

1. The normal maximum time for detention is 24 hours but this can be extended to 36 hours for indictable offences if it is authorised by an officer of the rank of superintendent or above.

2. For indictable offences applications can be made to the magistrates to extend the period up to a maximum of 96 hours.

3. Under the Terrorism Act 2006 a suspect can be detained for up to 14 days with the approval of a magistrate and up tp 28 days on application to a senior judge.

4. At the beginning of the period of detention the custody officer must inform the suspect of their rights to:
   - have someone informed of the arrest (s56 PACE);
   - legal advice in private (and that advice is available free of charge) (s58 PACE);
   - consult the Codes of Practice;
   - speak on the telephone for a reasonable time to one person (Code C).

The suspect must be given a written notice setting out these rights.

5. In the case of an indictable offence, where it is believed that it will hinder investigations the right to have someone informed and or hinder the recovery of property the right to legal advice can be delayed for up to 36 hours.

6. Where the suspect is under 17 years old, a parent or guardian should be notified of the detention (s34(2) Children and Young Persons Act 1933).

7. The custody officer is responsible for reviewing the detention and deciding whether the person should be detained. This must be done at the outset of the detention, then after six hours, then every nine hours (s40 PACE).

8. A record of all events (such as visits to the cell by police officers, or interviews) must be made by the custody officer.

8.4.2 The right to legal advice

1. Research in the early 1990s showed that only a small percentage of people detained requested legal advice. In order to try to make legal advice more available Code of Practice C now sets out that:
   - there must be a poster in each police station advertising the right to have legal advice;
   - police officers must not dissuade a person in detention from obtaining advice;
   - the custody officer must point out the right to legal advice and if the person declines to speak to a solicitor the custody officer must record the reason for the refusal.

2. Although the right to legal advice can be delayed for a maximum of 36 hours in the case of an indictable offence, the courts have held that it is only in rare cases that this right can be delayed (*R v Samuel* (1988), *R v Alladice* (1988)).

8.4.3 Interviews

1. At the start of an interview a suspect must be cautioned: 'You do not have to say anything. But it may harm your defence if you do not mention when questioned something which you later rely on in court. Anything you do say may be given in evidence'.

2. This caution emphasises that the right to silence was eroded by the Criminal Justice and Public Order Act 1994 which allows adverse inferences to be made at trial where the accused has failed in the police interview to mention facts (s34) or to account for objects, substances or marks (s36), or for his presence at a particular place (s37).

3. All interviews must be tape-recorded (s60 PACE).

4. Suspects are entitled to have a lawyer present during the interview, except where the right to legal advice has been delayed under s58 PACE in the case of an indictable offence (Code of Practice C).

5. Suspects under 17 or those who are mentally disordered or handicapped must have an appropriate adult present during the interview, even if they appear to understand the questions (*R v Aspinall* (1999)).

6. There should be a short break at least every two hours, breaks for meal times, and the suspect must be allowed an eight-hour period of rest.

7. Code of Practice E sets out rules and guidelines for the conduct of interviews.

8. If a confession is obtained by oppression or in circumstances likely to render it unreliable, this evidence can be excluded by the trial judge (s76 PACE).

8.4.4 Searches, samples and fingerprinting

1. When detained at a police station, a non-intimate search may be made if the custody office believes this is necessary (s54 PACE). The search must be carried out by a person of the same sex as the suspect.

2. If a strip search involving the removal of more than outer clothing is considered necessary, then the search must:

- take place where the suspect cannot be seen by any person who does not need to be present;
- be conducted with proper regard to the sensitivity of the person and to minimise embarrassment (Code of Practice C, Annex A).

3. An intimate search consists of the physical examination of a person's body orifices, other than the mouth.

4. An intimate search must be authorised by a superintendent or above in rank who believes that there is hidden:
   - an article which could cause harm; or
   - a Class A drug.

5. The actual search can only be carried out by a doctor or nurse, although, where it is for an article which may cause harm and a superintendent or above in rank considers it is not practicable to wait for a doctor or nurse, then a police officer may carry out the search.

6. Where the offence being investigated is a recordable offence, the police may take fingerprints (s60 PACE) and non-intimate samples, including hair (except pubic hair) and saliva (s63 PACE).

7. The consent of the person should be obtained before fingerprints or non-intimate samples are taken. If consent is refused fingerprints and non-intimate samples can be taken without consent where the person is detained or charged with a recordable offence. Reasonable force can be used if necessary (s117 PACE).

8. Intimate samples (blood, semen or any other tissue fluid, urine, pubic hair, a dental impression or a swab taken from a body orifice other than the mouth) can only be taken by a doctor or nurse (s62 PACE). Consent is needed.

9. At the moment any fingerprints or samples taken do not have to be destroyed even if the person is not found guilty or not even charged with any offence (s64 PACE as amended by the Criminal Justice and Police Act 2001).

10. In *R (S and Marper) v UK* (2008) the European Court of Justice ruled that the indefinite retention of samples of the innocent was a breach of human rights.

11. The Government has consulted on proposals that the retention would be limited to six years, but as yet the law has not been changed.

8.5 Complaints against the police

1. Any person who believes that the police have exceeded their powers may make a complaint to the police authorities.

2. The type of complaint determines how it is dealt with. Minor complaints may be informally resolved if the complainant agrees.

3. Any complaint which is not resolved must be referred to the Independent Police Complaints Commission (IPCC) which was set up by the Police Reform Act 2002.

4. When a case is referred to the IPCC, they decide how it should be investigated. The different methods of investigation are:
   - independent investigation carried out by the IPCC;
   - managed investigation carried out by the Professional Standards Department (PSD) of a police force under the direction and control of the IPCC;
   - supervised investigation by a PSD under their own direction and control but the IPCC sets the terms of reference and the PSD must report to the IPCC;
   - local investigation carried out entirely by a PSD.

8.5.1 Court actions against the police

1. Where there is an allegation that a police officer has committed a crime, eg assault, criminal proceedings may be taken against that police officer. These proceedings may be commenced by the Crown Prosecution Service or as a private prosecution by the victim.

2. Where there is a breach of civil rights, the individual affected may take civil proceedings and claim damages (compensation). For example, where the police have entered premises without a search warrant a claim for trespass to land may be made, or where there has been an unlawful arrest or unreasonable force a claim for trespass to the person may be made.

9

The criminal process and courts

Crown Prosecution Service

- Prosecution of Offences Act 1985
- Decide what offence to change
- Can discontinue if
  a) insufficient evidence
  b) not in public interest
- Glidewell Report (1998) critical; led to changes

Bail

Police bail

Bail granted by court
- Bail Act 1976
- Presumption in favour of bail
- Can refuse if believe would fail to surrender or commit offence or interfere with witnesses

CRIMINAL PROCESS

Criminal courts

Crown Court
- indictable offences
- tried by judge and jury

Magistrates' Court
- summary offences
- may send triable either way to Crown Court
- tried by a District Judge or lay magistrates

Appeals

From Magistrates to:
- Queen's Bench Divisional Court by case stated

OR
- Crown Court

From Crown Court to:
- Court of Appeal
- further appeal to Supreme Court

9.1 The Crown Prosecution Service (CPS)

1. The CPS was set up by the Prosecution of Offences Act 1985 as an independent prosecuting body. The head of the CPS is the Director of Public Prosecutions.

2. The CPS may later decide to discontinue a case if on further investigation there is insufficient evidence or if it is not in the public interest to prosecute.

3. The Code for Crown Prosecutors sets out some common public interest factors considered.

4. Factors in favour of prosecution include:
   - a weapon was used;
   - the defendant was in a position of authority or trust;
   - the offence was premeditated;
   - the offence was carried out by a group;
   - the defendant has relevant previous convictions.

5. Factors against prosecution include:
   - the offence was committed as a result of a genuine mistake;
   - the loss or harm is minor and arose from a single incident;
   - the defendant is elderly or suffering from significant mental or physical illness.

6. Following the Glidewell Report (1998) the CPS was reorganised into 42 areas with a chief Crown Prosecutor for each area.

7. In the Magistrates' Court the CPS will be represented by a Crown Prosecutor (qualified lawyer) or by an Associate Prosecutor (non-lawyer).

8. In the Crown Court, the CPS can be represented by a Crown Prosecutor who has the relevant advocacy qualification or by an independent advocate. Advocacy rights in the Crown Court were given to employed CPS lawyers by the Access to Justice Act 1999.

9.2 Bail

Bail can be given by the police or it can be given by a court before which the defendant appears.

1. There is a presumption that bail should be granted (s4 Bail Act 1976).

2. However, bail need not be granted where there are substantial grounds for believing that the accused would, if granted bail:
   - fail to surrender to custody;
   - commit an offence while on bail;
   - interfere with witnesses or otherwise obstruct the course of justice.

3. The court can also refuse to grant bail if it is satisfied that the defendant should be kept in custody for his own protection.

4. Factors considered include:
   - the nature and seriousness of the offence;
   - the character, antecedents, associations and community ties of the defendant;
   - the defendant's record of fulfilling his obligations under previous grants of bail;
   - the strength of the evidence against the defendant.

9.2.1 Special cases

1. The presumption in favour of bail is removed where it appears that the defendant has committed a triable either way offence or an indictable offence while on bail.

2. For murder, attempted murder, manslaughter, rape or attempted rape where the defendant has already served a custodial sentence for such an offence, bail should only be granted in exceptional circumstances (s56 Crime and Disorder Act 1998).

3. The prosecution may appeal against the grant of bail for any offence which carries a sentence of imprisonment.

9.2.2 Balancing conflicting interests

1. Individuals have a right to liberty (Human Rights Convention), but this right must be balanced against protection of the public. This balance must be considered when granting bail.

2. About 10% of those on bail commit further offences.

3. It is possible to use a curfew as a condition of bail, with electronic tagging to monitor those at risk of committing further offences.

4. About 10% of the prison population is in custody awaiting trial. Many of these are given non-custodial sentences or a very short prison sentence which means their immediate release. These defendants are

clearly not thought to be a danger to the public, but have had to stay in custody while awaiting trial.

9.3 Classification of offences

Summary offences	Triable either way offences	Indictable offences
Tried in Magistrates' Court Maximum sentence six months and/or £5,000 fine	Plea before venue • guilty plea – magistrates decide whether to hear case • not guilty plea – defendant has the right to elect trial by jury or stay in Magistrates' Court	First administrative hearing in Magistrates' Court Case then transferred to Crown Court • guilty plea – judge decides sentence • not guilty plea – jury decide verdict

The trial court is determined by the category of the offence being tried. There are three categories of offence. These are:
- summary – the least serious and can only be tried at a Magistrates' Court;
- triable either way – the middle range of offences and can be tried in either the Magistrates' Court or the Crown Court;
- indictable – the most serious offences and can only be tried at the Crown Court.

9.4 Magistrates' Court

9.4.1 Jurisdiction of the Magistrates' Court

1. Tries all summary offences and any offence triable either way where both the magistrates and the defendant agree to it being tried in the Magistrates' Courts.

2. These two categories account for about 97% of all criminal cases and in about 90% of these the defendants plead guilty.

3. The maximum sentence in the Magistrates' Courts is six months' imprisonment for one offence (12 months for two offences) and a fine of £5,000.

4. Conducts plea before venue hearings in respect of all triable either way offences. Any defendant who pleads guilty will then be dealt with in the Magistrates' Court.

5. Where a defendant pleads not guilty to a triable either way offence, a mode of trial hearing will then be held to decide whether the case should be tried in the Magistrates' Court or the Crown Court.

6. Deals with the first hearing of all indictable offences; these cases are then sent to the Crown Court.

7. Decides whether to grant arrest warrants or search warrants, and whether the defendant should be granted bail.

8. Youth Court hears cases involving those aged 10 to 17 inclusive.

9. The Magistrates' Court also has civil jurisdiction. This includes:
   - hearing appeals against a local authority's refusal to grant licences to pubs or other venues to sell alcohol;
   - enforcing demands for council tax;
   - hearing family cases;
   - proceedings under the Children Act 1989.

9.4.2 The Youth Court

1. Young offenders aged 10 to 17 inclusive are tried here. The exception is young offenders charged with very serious offences including murder, manslaughter, rape, or causing death by dangerous driving, who must be tried at the Crown Court. In addition, other serious offences (carrying a sentence of 14 years' imprisonment or more for an adult) may be tried in the Crown Court.

2. There must be three magistrates on the bench, with a mix of sexes, and the magistrates in the Youth Court have special training.

3. The procedure is less formal than in the adult court, with only authorised persons present.

4. A parent or guardian must be present where the offender is under 16, unless it would be unreasonable to require such attendance in the circumstances.

9.5 Appeals from the Magistrates' Court

Supreme Court

permission to appeal
point of law of general
public importance

Queen's Bench Divisional Court

case stated
appeal

Crown Court

retrial
defence only

Magistrates' Court

There are two different appeal routes.

1. Case stated appeal to the Queen's Bench Divisional Court (QBD).

   a) This is used where the appeal is on a point of law – the magistrates are asked to state a case (finding of facts). The QBD can quash the decision, confirm it or remit the case to the Magistrates' Court for a re-hearing.

   b) This route is available for both prosecution and defence.

   c) A further appeal is possible to the Supreme Court. This must be on a point of law of general public importance and the Supreme Court (or QBD) must give permission to appeal. This is only used a few times each year.

2. The Crown Court.

   a) This route is only available to the defendant. The appeal can be on sentence or conviction or both.

   b) The whole case is reheard at the Crown Court by a judge and two lay magistrates.

   c) There is no further appeal, unless a point of law is involved when the appeal then goes to the QBD as above.

9.6 The Crown Court

1. The Crown Court sits in about 90 centres.

2. Once a case has been transferred from the Magistrates' Court, a plea and directions hearing will be held to establish whether the plea is guilty or not guilty and to identify key issues for the trial.

3. If the defendant pleads guilty, the judge will decide the sentence.

4. If the defendant pleads not guilty, the trial is held before a judge and a jury of 12. The judge decides the law and the jury decides the facts. The jury decides whether the defendant is guilty or not guilty. This can be by a unanimous verdict or by a majority verdict (11 to 1 or 10 to 2).

9.7 Appeals from the Crown Court

Supreme Court

permission to appeal
point of law of general
public importance

Court of Appeal

(Criminal Division)

prosecution against
unduly lenient sentence

defence against
sentence/conviction

A-G's reference
on point of law

Crown Court

The defendant may appeal against conviction and/or sentence. The prosecution has limited rights of appeal against conviction and sentence.

9.7.1 Appeals by the defendant

1. The defendant may appeal against conviction and/or sentence to the Court of Appeal (Criminal Division). In all cases the defendant needs leave to appeal from the Court of Appeal, or the trial judge must grant a certificate that the case is fit for appeal.

2. The only ground for allowing an appeal against conviction is that the conviction is unsafe (s2(1) Criminal Appeal Act 1968 as amended by the Criminal Appeal Act 1995).

3. If the Court of Appeal allows the defendant's appeal, it may order a retrial (s7 Criminal Appeal Act 1968 as amended by the Criminal Justice Act 1988) or it may quash the conviction.

4. When hearing an appeal, the Court of Appeal has power to admit fresh evidence if it is necessary or expedient in the interests of justice (s23(1) Criminal Appeal Act 1968).

9.7 2 Appeals by the prosecution

1. The prosecution may apply to the High Court for an order to quash an acquittal because of interference with a witness or the jury (s54 Criminal Procedure and Investigations Act 1996).

2. Following an acquittal the Attorney-General may refer a point of law to the Court of Appeal (Criminal Division). This does not affect the acquittal; it merely states the law for future cases (s36 Criminal Justice Act 1972).

3. The Criminal Justice Act 2003 allows the prosecution to appeal in respect of a ruling made by the trial judge on a point of law. The trial can be adjourned for the appeal to be decided. This will prevent defendants from being acquitted because the judge has made an error of law.

4. For serious offences such as murder and rape, the prosecution may apply to the Court of Appeal for an acquittal to be quashed and a re-trial to be ordered. This can only be done where there is new and compelling evidence that the defendant is guilty and it is in the interests of justice to hold a re-trial (ss76–83 Criminal Justice Act 2003).

5. The Attorney-General may (with leave from the Court of Appeal) refer an unduly lenient sentence to the Court of Appeal for them to review the sentence (s36 Criminal Justice Act 1988). The Court of Appeal can quash the original sentence and impose a more severe sentence.

9.7.3 Appeals to the House of Lords

1. Both the prosecution and the defence have the right to appeal from the Court of Appeal (Criminal Division) to the Supreme Court.

2. In any case the Court of Appeal must have certified that the case involves a point of law of general public importance, and either the Court of Appeal or the Supreme Court must give leave to appeal (s33(2) Criminal Appeal Act 1968).

3. There is no appeal to the Supreme Court on sentence.

9.8 Miscarriages of justice

9.8.1 The Criminal Case Review Commission

1. The Criminal Case Review Commission (CCRC) was set up in 1997 under the Criminal Appeal Act 1995.

2. Prior to this the responsibility for referring possible miscarriages of justice back to the Court of Appeal lay with the Home Secretary. This was criticised as being too involved with the Executive and an ineffective method of dealing with possible miscarriages of justice.

3. The CCRC can investigate cases which were tried in the Crown Court or the Magistrates' Court. Where the case was tried in the Crown Court it may be referred to the Court of Appeal; where the trial was in the Magistrates' Court, the referral is to the Crown Court.

4. The CCRC can only refer a case if:
   - an appeal has been decided or leave to appeal has been refused; and
   - it considers there is a real possibility that the conviction (or sentence) would not be upheld (s13 Criminal Appeal Act 1995).

10

Sentencing

Sentencing aims

- Retribution
- Deterrence
- Protection/incapacitation
- Rehabilitation
- Reparation
- Denunciation

SENTENCING

Special powers for young offenders

- Detention and training orders
- Youth Rehabilitation order with requirements. e.g.
  a) attendance centre
  b) supervision
  c) action plan
  d) reparation
- Reprimands/warnings
- Referral to Youth Offending Panels

Sentences available

- Custodial
- Community order with requirements, eg:
  a) supervision
  b) unpaid work
  c) curfew
  d) drug treatment
- Fines
- Conditional/absolute discharge

1. A distinguishing feature of the criminal law is that there is the possibility of the State imposing a punishment on an offender. Hart's definition of 'punishment' is that it must:
   - involve pain or other unpleasant consequences;
   - be for an offence against legal rules;
   - be intentionally administered by human beings other than the offender;
   - be imposed and administered by an authority constituted by a legal system against which the offence is committed.

2. Before punishment is imposed, the sentencer should consider which aim(s) of sentencing to use, background factors (reports, etc) and the sentences available.

10.1 Aims of sentencing

1. These are concerned with the purpose or objective that the sentencer or policy-maker is seeking to achieve.

2. There are different sentencing aims that recognise the different needs of the offender, the victim and society. These needs may be in conflict.

3. Changes in penal policies can lead to one or more sentencing aims being preferred over others.

4. The purposes of sentencing are now set out in statute (s142 Criminal Justice Act 2003). For offenders 18 and over the court must have regard to:
   - the punishment of offenders;
   - the reduction of crime (including its reduction by deterrence);
   - the reform and rehabilitation of offenders;
   - the protection of the public; and
   - the making of reparation by offenders to persons affected by their offences.

5. For offenders under the age of 18, the purposes of sentencing are set out in s142A Criminal Justice Act 2003. They are:
   - the punishment of offenders;
   - the reform and rehabilitation of offenders;
   - the protection of the public; and
   - the making of reparation by offenders to persons affected by their offences.

6. In addition the court must have regard *primarily* to the principal aim of the youth justice system to prevent offending and must also consider the welfare of the offender.

10.1.1 Punishment

1. Punishment is also referred to as retribution. It is thought of as being 'an eye for an eye and a tooth for a tooth', and society's revenge for the offence.

2. Its literal form is in the death penalty for murder: a life for a life. A literal interpretation is not practical for most offences and the aim is to 'let the punishment fit the crime'.

3. Retribution is based on blameworthiness, so a mentally ill offender should not be subjected to retribution.

4. Retribution is also based on proportionality or 'just desserts', so that the sentence reflects the seriousness of the offence. This concept is supported by the use of tariff sentences and guidelines issued by the Sentencing Guidelines Council.

5. Retribution can be seen in our sentencing legislation which states that a court must not pass a custodial sentence unless the offence was so serious that only a custodial sentence can be justified for the offence (s152(2) Criminal Justice Act 2003 (CJA)).

10.1.2 Deterrence

1. There are two forms of deterrence:
   ■ individual deterrence;
   ■ general deterrence.

2. Individual deterrence is aimed at the particular offender. It aims to make the experience of punishment so unpleasant that the individual will not re-offend. Alternatively a threat (such as a suspended sentence) is used to deter.

3. General deterrence is aimed at discouraging others from committing that type of offence.

4. Deterrence is based on the assumption that potential offenders will consider the consequences of their actions. In fact, most offences are committed on the spur of the moment, so any deterrent effect is minimal.

5. Deterrence is not concerned with fairness or proportionality; the sentence imposed, especially for general deterrence, is likely to be harsher than the normal tariff for the offence.

10.1.3 Protection of society

1. This is usually achieved by incapacitation of the offender so that he or she cannot commit further offences. The ultimate example is the death penalty.

2. The sentence used to achieve incapacitation may be more severe than that needed for retribution. This conflict has been called 'deservedness versus dangerousness' (*von Hirsch*).

3. In our penal system a long custodial sentence is the usual method of incapacitation.

4. Section 225 of the Criminal Justice Act 2003 sets out that life imprisonment can be given where an offender has committed a serious violent or sexual offence and there is a significant risk of harm to the public from further offending.

5. There are other sentences which rely on incapacitation. For example, disqualification from driving; or disqualification from owning an animal for an offence of cruelty.

6. Electronic tagging gives a degree of incapacitation while allowing the offender to remain in the community.

10.1.4 Rehabilitation

1. This aims to reform the offender and so reduce the likelihood of future re-offending.

2. A sentence aimed at rehabilitation is considered an individualised sentence as opposed to the tariff sentences given under the retributive aim. Individualised sentences can lead to apparent inconsistency in sentencing.

3. It is now accepted that imprisonment has only limited rehabilitative effect.

4. The Criminal Justice Act 2003 provides for a community order to be made with requirements attached to it. The court can specify any requirements which it thinks will help in rehabilitating the offender. (The possible requirements are listed at 10.2.3.)

5. These requirements have been developed as studies of re-offending rates showed that those placed on probation with no additional requirements were almost as likely to re-offend as those given custodial sentences.

6. Rehabilitation is particularly important for young offenders to try to break the cycle of re-offending.

10.1.5 Reparation or restitution

1. There has been increasing concern that victims are not adequately considered when sentencing the offender.

2. Compensation orders are used instead of or in addition to the sentence imposed on the offender as reparation to the victim.

3. If the court does not make a compensation order when it has power to do so, then it must give reasons for not doing so (s130 Powers of Criminal Courts (Sentencing) Act 2000 (PCC(S)A)).

4. Unpaid work requirements involve the offender doing a certain number of hours' work on community projects. This has an element of reparation to society at large.

5. An activity requirement in a community order can contain an element of reparation where the court thinks this is suitable.

6. A reparation order can be made where the offender is under 18. This can order reparation to the victim or the community at large (s73 PCC(S)A).

10.1.6 Denunciation

1. Although denunciation is not referred to in the purposes of sentencing in the Criminal Justice Act 2003, theorists recognise it as an aim of sentencing.

2. This is expressing society's outrage at the offence committed.

3. It emphasises the criminality of the offence, but it goes beyond retribution in that society's expectations are also considered.

4. Denunciation is the main aim behind long prison sentences being imposed for offences of causing death by dangerous driving.

5. Failure by the courts to punish in accordance with society's expectations may lead to people taking action themselves, eg vigilantes.

10.2 Types of sentences

10.2.1 Custodial sentences

1. Murder carries a mandatory sentence of life imprisonment for offenders aged 18 and over. Offenders under 18 who are convicted of murder are detained at Her Majesty's pleasure (s90 PCC(S)A). The minimum term to be served is governed by Schedule 22 of the Criminal Justice Act 2003.

2. For other offences a prison sentence up to the maximum for the particular offence can be imposed on offenders aged 18 and over. Offenders under 18 who are convicted of serious offences may be detained for a set period up to the maximum for the offence.

3. Under s225 Criminal Justice Act 2003 a life sentence or imprisonment for public protection, which is for an indeterminate period, can be given to an offender who commits a serious violent or sexual offence.

4. Under s227 Criminal Justice Act 2003 an offender who commits a less serious violent or sexual offence can be given an extended sentence. The period of extension is served on licence in the community. This period can be up to five years for a violent offence and up to eight years for a sexual offence.

5. A term of imprisonment for less than 12 months is known as 'custody plus'. This is because the offender will serve part of the time in prison and then the remainder on licence with requirements attached.

6. The Criminal Justice Act 2003 introduced the concept of intermittent custody but this was abolished in 2007.

7. Offenders aged 18–20 may serve their sentence in a prison or Young Offenders Institution (s61 Criminal Justice and Court Services Act 2000).

8. Offenders aged 12–17 can be sentenced to a detention and training order for a specified period of between four and 24 months. For those under 15 years old such an order can only be made if the offender is a persistent offender (s100 PCC(S)A).

10.2.2 Minimum sentences

1. Offenders convicted of a third offence of class A drug trafficking must be sentenced to a minimum of seven years' imprisonment (s110 PCC(S) A).

2. Offenders convicted of a third offence of burglary must be sentenced to a minimum of three years' imprisonment (s111 PCC(S)A).

10.2.3 Community orders

1. The Government emphasis has been on extending the types of community sentences available and on making them 'tougher' so that they are not seen as a soft option.

2. Section 177(1) of the Criminal Justice Act 2003 allows a court to impose on defendants aged 16 or over, as part of a community order, any one or more of the following requirements:

   a) an unpaid work requirement;

   b) an activity requirement;

   c) a programme requirement;

   d) a prohibited activity requirement;

   e) a curfew requirement;

   f) an exclusion requirement;

   g) a residence requirement;

   h) a mental health treatment requirement;

   i) a drug rehabilitation requirement;

   j) an alcohol treatment requirement;

   k) a supervision requirement; and

   l) in the case where the offender is aged under 25, an attendance centre requirement.

3. The court can only impose a mental health treatment requirement, a drug rehabilitation requirement or an alcohol treatment requirement where the defendant expresses his willingness to comply with the requirement.

10.3 Other powers of the court

1. A fine can be imposed for any offence. There is no limit to the amount which the Crown Court can fine an offender. The maximum fine in the Magistrates' Court is £5,000, except for health and safety offences where it is £20,000.

2. There are limits on the amount young offenders can be fined:
   - 10–13 year olds: maximum £250;
   - 14–17 year olds: maximum £1,000.

3. A conditional discharge may be given for a period of up to three years on the condition that during this time the offender does not re-offend (s12 PCC(S)A).

4. An absolute discharge may be given. This has no conditions attached; the matter is at an end.

5. Disqualification from driving can be ordered for driving offences and also for non-driving offences, eg theft (s146 PCC(S)A).

10.4 Additional powers in respect of young offenders (10–17)

1. A youth rehabilitation order can be made with various requirements.

2. The requirements under a youth rehabilitation order are similar to those for adults but also include a local authority residence requirement and an education requirement.

3. A reprimand or a warning may be given. These are not sentences imposed by a court. They are methods by which the police may deal with a young offender without taking the case to court.

4. Referral to a youth offender team must be ordered where an offender who has no previous convictions has pleaded guilty to an offence in court. Referral is also obligatory after a warning.

5. An offender's parent or guardian may be bound over for a period of up to three years to take proper care and exercise proper control of the offender (s150 PCC(S)A).

6. A parenting order requiring parents to attend counselling or guidance sessions can be made when an offender under the age of 18 is convicted of an offence. The order is also available in civil proceedings where the court makes a child safety order or an anti-social behaviour order (s8 Crime and Disorder Act 1998).

10.5 Mentally ill offenders

1. In addition to the normal range of penalties there are special powers available to the court to deal with an offender who is mentally ill.

2. The main powers are:
   - to add a requirement to a community order that the offender attends for treatment; or
   - to make a hospital order to enable the offender to receive appropriate treatment as an in-patient; or
   - where the offender is a danger to the community, to make a restriction order sending the offender to a secure hospital (s41 Mental Health Act 1983).

10.6 Other factors in sentencing

10.6.1 Factors surrounding the offence

1. The level of seriousness of the offence within its type is important, eg the amount stolen, the seriousness of injuries inflicted, the type of weapon used.

2. Other factors that aggravate an offence include:
   - premeditation;
   - a vulnerable victim;
   - an abuse of trust;
   - being the ring leader;
   - racial or religious hostility (s145 CJA);
   - hostility based on sexual orientation or disability (s146 CJA).

3. Where the offender has pleaded not guilty, these facts will have been given as part of the evidence.

4. Where the offender has pleaded guilty, the facts of the case are outlined to the court by the prosecution. If the defendant does not agree with the prosecution's version, then a Newton hearing is held to establish the facts.

10.6.2 The offender's background

1. Previous convictions of the offender or any failure to respond to previous sentences may be taken into account in considering the seriousness of the offence.

2. Pre-sentence reports on the offender and his background may be available for the court.

3. The stage in the court proceedings at which the defendant pleaded guilty to the offence is considered.

4. The Sentencing Guidelines Council guidelines are that where the defendant pleaded guilty at the first reasonable opportunity there should be a reduction of up to one third, whereas a plea of guilty after the trial has started would only be given a one tenth reduction. The amount of reduction is on a sliding scale as shown in the diagram below.

5. If the evidence is overwhelming, then the reduction for a guilty plea is limited to 20%.

Stage in the proceedings

First reasonable opportunity / After trial set / Door of court or after trial has begun

No reduction

1/3 (20% if evidence overwhelming) / 1/4 / up to 1/10

Proportionate reduction

10.7 Anti-social behaviour orders

1. These orders (ASBOs) are civil orders, not criminal penalties.

2. They can be imposed when a person has behaved in an anti-social manner.

3. The type of behaviour included under the term 'anti-social' is very wide, eg harassment or being frequently drunk or high on drugs and causing a nuisance in public or to neighbours.

4. Under an ASBO the person can be ordered not to go to certain areas or take part in certain types of behaviour.

5. Breaking an ASBO is a criminal matter and the offender can then be sentenced for the breach.

6. This has been criticised as custodial orders are being imposed on defendants who are in breach of an ASBO, even though they could not have been imprisoned for the behaviour for which the ASBO was imposed.

7. There is also the criticism that ASBOs are imposed on mentally ill people. This is inappropriate as such people require treatment for their behaviour and without treatment are likely to breach the ASBO and be put at risk of imprisonment.

8. In addition, the imposition of ASBOs is often publicised, even for juvenile offenders whose names would be withheld in a criminal case.

9. In *R (Stanley, Marshall and Kelly) v Metropolitan Commander and others* (2004) the Divisional Court held that publishing names was not an infringement of Article 8(1) of the European Convention on Human Rights (right to privacy), provided that the publicity was necessary and proportionate to a legitimate aim, such as the need to protect the community.

10. The intention of ASBOs is both to protect the community and to try to prevent the person's behaviour from deteriorating further into truly criminal activity.

11

The legal profession

LEGAL PROFESSION

SOLICITORS
Training

BARRISTERS
Training

Degree, if not in law then must do
Graduate Diploma in Law

- Legal Practice Course
- Training contract

- Bar Professional Training
  Course
- Pupillage

Role

- Private practice in solicitors' firm
- Wide variety of work
- Contracts, leases, wills
  conveyancing etc.
- Direct access by clients

Role

- Self-employed in chambers
- Mostly court work
- Also write opinions and draft
  documents
- Direct access in civil cases only

May be employed in CPS, CDS, local
authority, etc or private commercial business

Advocacy rights

Advocacy certificate
(Courts and Legal
Services Act 1990)
Provision for full rights
(Access to Justice Act 1999)

Advocacy rights

Full rights

Supervision

Law Society

Supervision

Bar Council

Legal Services Ombudsman

11.1 Solicitors

11.1.1 Training

1. To become a solicitor it is usual to have a law degree which covers the seven core subjects of:
   - contract law;
   - law of torts;
   - criminal law;
   - land law;
   - equity and trusts;
   - constitutional and administrative law;
   - European Union law.

If a student has a degree in another subject it is necessary to take the Graduate Diploma in Law.

1. The next stage is the one-year Legal Practice Course (LPC), which includes training in skills such as client interviewing, negotiation and advocacy.

2. After passing this the student must then obtain a training contract. This can be with a firm of solicitors, or in an organisation such as the Crown Prosecution Service (CPS) or the legal department of a local authority. The training contract is for a period of two years and gives the trainee solicitor practical experience.

3. A 20-day Professional Skills Course must be completed during the training period.

4. After completing all the above the trainee will be admitted as a solicitor by the Law Society.

5. There is also a route for non-graduate mature students to qualify. This is by becoming a fellow of the Institute of Legal Executives (must be over 25 years, have passed Part I and Part II ILEX examinations and have worked in a solicitor's office for at least five years). They must then take the LPC examinations.

11.1.2 Role

1. The majority of those who qualify as solicitors will work in private practice in a solicitor's firm.

2. Initially they will work as an assistant solicitor in a firm, but may eventually become a partner or set up on their own as a sole practitioner.

3. There is no maximum on the number of partners in a firm of solicitors. The size of firms varies from the sole practitioner to partnerships with over 100 partners and several hundred assistant solicitors.

4. The work of a solicitor will vary according to the type of firm. Small high street firms are likely to concentrate on family law, wills and probate, housing law, consumer law and criminal law. Large city firms specialise in business and commercial law.

5. Other careers are available as an employed lawyer in an organisation such as the CPS, Civil Service or local authority. Solicitors are also employed by private businesses as legal advisers.

11.1.3 Advocacy rights

1. Solicitors in private practice can also act as advocates. They have always had full advocacy rights in the Magistrates' Court and the County Court.

2. The Courts and Legal Services Act 1990 allowed them to apply for an advocacy certificate for rights in the higher courts, but only about 5% have applied for a certificate.

3. The Access to Justice Act 1999 provided that all solicitors will be given full rights of audience. The intention was to bring in new training requirements to ensure that newly qualified solicitors will automatically have advocacy rights but this has not yet happened.

4. Solicitors employed by the CPS may act as a prosecutor-advocate in any court for which they hold an advocacy qualification.

5. Solicitors employed by the Legal Services Commission may act as an advocate to represent members of the public in any court for which they hold an advocacy qualification.

6. Other employed solicitors only have rights of audience to represent their employer.

11.2 Barristers

11.2.1 Training

1. To qualify as a barrister it is usual to have a law degree. If a student has a degree in another subject then it is necessary to take the Graduate Diploma in Law.

2. Would-be barristers must then take the Bar Professional Training Course (BPTC), which places emphasis on practical skills of drafting pleadings and advocacy.

3. All students must also become a member of one of the four Inns of Court and must either dine at that Inn a set number of times or attend weekend courses run by the Inn.

4. After passing the BPTC and completing the necessary attendance at an Inn of Court, the person is called to the Bar and is officially qualified as a barrister. However, before they can appear in court they must do a 12-month period of pupillage, 'work-shadowing' a barrister.

11.2.2 Role

1. Barristers at the Bar are self-employed. They usually practise from chambers, sharing expenses of rent, secretarial staff, etc.

2. They are independent and can be briefed by any solicitor. In addition, in civil cases, they can be approached directly by the public.

3. Members of the public used to have to brief a barrister via a solicitor. However, direct access by the public is now allowed in civil cases.

4. The majority of barristers concentrate on advocacy and they have rights of audience in all courts. Their other work involves giving advice and opinions on points of law or potential cases and drafting papers for court.

5. Some barristers specialising in areas such as taxation or patent law will rarely appear in court.

6. Employed barristers can work for the CPS, government departments, local authorities or businesses. Employed barristers now retain their rights of audience though there are limits on who they may represent (Access to Justice Act 1999).

11.3 Queen's Counsel

1. After being qualified for ten years a barrister or solicitor may apply to 'take silk' and become a Queen's Counsel (QC).

2. Selection of who should become a QC is now made by an independent selection panel.

3. Lawyers apply to become QCs. They have to pay a fee. They are interviewed by members of the panel. Applicants provide references (these can include references from clients).

4. The panel then recommends those who should be appointed to the Lord Chancellor.

11.4 Para-legals

11.4.1 Legal executives

1. To become a Fellow of the Institute of Legal Executives (ILEX) it is necessary to be over 25 years of age, to have passed the ILEX Part I and Part II examinations and to have worked in a solicitor's firm (or other comparable employment, eg CPS) for at least five years.

2. Legal executives work in solicitors' firms and deal with the more straightforward cases.

3. They have limited rights of audience in the County Court to make unopposed applications.

11.4.2 Licensed conveyancers

1. These specialise in the conveyancing of property.

2. Complaints about licensed conveyancers are dealt with by the Legal Services Ombudsman.

11.5 Regulation of the legal professions

11.5.1 The Law Society

1. This is the governing body of solicitors.

2. It is a regulatory body that can set rules and discipline solicitors.

3. It also acts as the representative of the interests of solicitors.

4. There have been frequent problems of delay and inefficiency with complaints handling by the Law Society over a long period of time.

5. In order to make the complaints procedure more independent of the Law Society, the Consumer Complaints Service was set up in 2004 with lay members as part of the panel.

6. Although there has been some improvement, the Legal Services Ombudsman's annual reports still show that about one third of complaints are not handled satisfactorily.

7. In 2006 the Legal Services Complaints Commissioner fined the Law Society £250,000 for submitting an inadequate complaints-handling plan for the following year.

8. Serious complaints against solicitors are heard by the Solicitors Disciplinary Council. This Council has the power to strike off solicitors.

11.5.2 The Bar Council

1. This is the governing body of barristers.

2. As with the Law Society, it has both regulatory and representative functions.

3. Complaints against barristers are handled by the Bar Standards Board. If there was poor service, the Board can order the barrister to pay compensation of up to £15,000 to the client.

4. The complaints process is overseen by an independent Lay Complaints Commissioner.

5. The Legal Services Ombudsman's annual reports show that about 90% of complaints are handled satisfactorily.

6. The Senate of the Inns of Court will hear serious complaints and has the power to disbar a barrister.

11.5.3 The Legal Services Ombudsman

1. The post of Legal Services Ombudsman was set up by the Courts and Legal Services Act 1990.

2. The Ombudsman oversees solicitors, barristers and licensed conveyancers.

3. The Ombudsman investigates whether complaints have been properly handled by the regulatory bodies.

4. The Access to Justice Act 1999 gave the Ombudsman power to order payment of compensation by an individual lawyer or firm.

11.5.4 Suing a lawyer

1. There is a contract between a solicitor and client. So, if there is a breach of contract, the client has the right to sue the solicitor. There is no contract between a client and their barrister.

2. It is possible for a client to sue both solicitors and barristers for negligence. In some cases where the negligence has caused loss to a third person, that person may be able to sue (*White v Jones* (1995)).

3. It used not to be possible to sue either a barrister or a solicitor for negligent advocacy (*Rondel v Worsley* (1969), *Saif Ali v Sydney Mitchell and Co* (1980)). However, this rule was changed in the case of *Hall v Simons* (2000) and it is now possible to sue for negligent advocacy.

11.6 Legal Services Act 2007

11.6.1 Regulation of the legal profession

1. The Act creates the Legal Services Board (LSB).

2. It consists of a Chairman and seven to ten members. The first Chairman must be a non-lawyer and the majority of members must also be non-lawyers

3. The role of the Board is to have independent oversight regulation of the legal profession.

4. Primary responsibility for regulation rests with the Law Society and Bar Council and the LSB should only interfere when their actions are palpably unreasonable.

11.6.2 Complaints against the legal profession

1. The Act provides for the setting up of the Office for Legal Complaints (OCL) which will deal with complaints against all lawyers and para-legals. It will begin operating in 2010.

2. It has been estimated that between 80% and 90% of Law Society staff from the Consumer Complaints Service will transfer to the Office for Legal Complaints.

3. Both the Bar Council and the Legal Services Ombudsman have expressed concern over this, because of the Law Society's record of poor complaint handling.

11.6.3 Alternative business structures (ABSs)

1. The Act allows legal businesses to:
   - include lawyers and non-lawyers
   - include barristers and solicitors
   - be owned by non-lawyers
   - be operated as companies.

2. ABSs will be introduced in 2011.

3. In deciding on giving licences to operate ABSs, access to justice must be properly considered.

4. The Law Society will be able to approve Legal Disciplinary Practices (partnerships containing solicitors, barristers and non-lawyers) in advance of the full introduction of ABSs.

12

The Judiciary

Superior judges

- Justices of the Supreme Court
- Lords Justices of Appeal
- High Court Judges
- Selection by Judicial Appointments Commission
- Appointed by monarch
- Security of tenure
- Largely white/male

Inferior judges

- District Judges
- Recorders
- Circuit Judges
- Posts advertised: applicants interviewed
- Appointment by monarch
- Increasing number of women and ethnic minorities

JUDICIARY

Independence of judiciary

- Separation of powers
- Immunity from suit
- Superior judges have security of tenure

But

- 'Conservative'
- White/male dominated
- Public school/Oxbridge dominated

Lord Chancellor

- Appointed by Prime Minister
- Role is in conflict with separation of powers
- Involvement in judicial appointments
- Responsible for courts and funding
- Responsible for many other public offices

Judges can be divided into two main types: inferior judges and superior judges. These categories affect the way judges are appointed, the courts they sit in and the way they can be dismissed.

12.1 Appointment

1. The professional qualifications needed to become a judge are set out in the Courts and Legal Services Act 1990 as amended by the Tribunals, Court and Enforcement Act 2007. To be appointed it is necessary to have a legal qualification and to have gained experience in the law for a certain period of time.

2. Up to 2005 the Lord Chancellor played a major part in selecting and recommending judges for appointment.

3. Since 2005 the selection of judges has been by the Judicial Appointments Commission.

12.1.1 The Judicial Appointments Commission

1. This was set up under the Constitutional Reform Act 2005.

2. There are 15 members of this Commission:
   - 6 lay members;
   - 5 judges – 3 of these to be from the Court of Appeal or High Court plus 1 circuit judge and 1 district judge or equivalent;
   - 1 barrister, 1 solicitor, 1 magistrate and 1 tribunal member.

3. All judicial vacancies are advertised. Candidates must apply.

4. All selection is based entirely on merit.

5. The Commission will recommend to the Lord Chancellor who should be appointed.

6. The Lord Chancellor has limited powers in relation to each recommendation for appointment. He is able to reject a candidate once or ask the Commission to reconsider once and, in doing so, he must provide reasons.

7. Once the Lord Chancellor has accepted the recommendations, all judges are then appointed by the Monarch.

12.1.2 Inferior judges

1. District Judges sit in the County Court and Magistrates' Court. They:
   - must be qualified as a barrister or solicitor and have gained experience in law for at least five years or to have been a Deputy District Judge;
   - Deputy District Judges can also be appointed from those qualified as an ILEX Fellow.

2. Recorders are part-time judges who can sit in the County Court and the Crown Court. They:
   - must be qualified as a barrister or solicitor and have gained experience in law for at least seven years;
   - are appointed for a renewable period of five years;
   - must sit for at least 15–30 days per year.

The five-year term of office and the abolition of the post of Assistant Recorder were announced in 2000. This was to try to ensure that judges would be considered sufficiently independent of the Executive for the purposes of the European Convention on Human Rights (*Starrs v Procurator Fiscal* (1999)).

3. Circuit Judges are full-time judges who sit in the County Court and/or Crown Court. They:
   - must be qualified as a barrister or solicitor and have gained experience in law for at least seven years or have been a Recorder or District Judge.

12.1.3 Superior judges

1. High Court Judges or Puisne Judges sit in the High Court. They will be appointed to one of the three divisions (Queen's Bench, Chancery or Family). They:
   - must be qualified as a barrister or solicitor and have gained experience in law for at least seven years or have been a Circuit Judge for at least two years;
   - will usually have sat as a Deputy High Court judge before being appointed.

2. Lords Justices of Appeal sit in the Court of Appeal and must be qualified as a barrister or solicitor and have gained experience in law for at least seven years or be an existing High Court Judge.

3. Justices of the Supreme Court must have been qualified to appear in senior courts for at least 15 years or have held high judicial office in England and Wales or Scotland or Northern Ireland for at least two years.

12.1.4 Criticism of the appointment system

1. The Lord Chancellor has had too much influence in appointments, it was felt that reform was needed.

2. The old system had an emphasis on the 'old boy' network, with the use of secret soundings.

3. The old boy network showed in the fact that the majority of new appointments for High Court Judges came from sets of barristers where ex-members were judges.

4. There have been only three solicitors appointed to the High Court Bench; one of these has since been appointed to the Court of Appeal.

5. There are only a small number of women judges, especially in the High Court and above. It was not until 2004 that the first woman judge was appointed to the House of Lords and is now in the Supreme Court.

6. The number of judges from ethnic minorities is very small – less than 3% of Circuit Judges. The first ethnic minority judge in the High Court was appointed in 2004.

7. Under the new appointments system there are more women and ethnic minority judges being appointed to the lower levels of the judiciary. However, most appointments to the higher levels of the judiciary have been of white males.

12.2 Training

1. This is organised by the Judicial Studies Board (JSB).

2. For most new judges there is a short residential course (three or four days).

3. New Recorders also have to visit two penal establishments and sit in on trials at a Crown Court.

4. Most judges will attend a continuation seminar once every three years.

5. There are additional special training schemes for new areas of law such as the introduction of the Human Rights Act 1998.

6. Part-time judges are subject to appraisal schemes.

7. There is criticism that the training of judges is inadequate, in particular that the initial course for Recorders is too short, as lawyers who are not criminal law practitioners will be expected to sit on criminal cases.

12.3 Removal

1. It is seen as important that judges should be independent, so they must be protected from removal at the whim of the Government.

2. As a result, superior judges have security of tenure that dates back to the Act of Settlement 1701. They can only be removed by the Monarch following a petition presented by both Houses of Parliament.

3. The Lord Chancellor can, after consultation with the Lord Chief Justice, declare vacant the office of any judge who, through ill-health, is incapable of carrying out his work and of taking the decision to resign.

4. Inferior judges can be dismissed by the Lord Chancellor for incapacity or misbehaviour (s17(4) Courts Act 1971), but only if the Lord Chief Justice consents to the dismissal.

12.4 Independence of the Judiciary

12.4.1 Doctrine of the separation of powers

1. This doctrine was first put forward by Montesquieu in the eighteenth century.

2. The theory is that the three primary functions of the State (Legislature, Executive and Judiciary) must be kept separate in order to safeguard the rights of citizens.

3. In our Government the Legislature is Parliament, the Executive is the Cabinet and the Judiciary is the judges.

4. There is an overlap of the Legislature and Executive as the Cabinet are also members of Parliament.

5. The Lord Chancellor's role goes across all three arms of State.

6. The judges on the Judicial Committee of the House of Lords used to sit in the House of Lords in a legislative capacity. However, this ceased when the Judicial Committee of the House of Lords was replaced by the Supreme Court.

12.4.2 The Judiciary

1. The Lord Chancellor is appointed by the Prime Minister and holds office only while the Prime Minister wishes.

2. The Lord Chancellor still plays a small role in recommending judicial appointments. This is contrary to the doctrine of separation of powers.

3. Section 3 of the Constitutional Reform Act 2005 guarantees the principle of judicial independence. It states that the Lord Chancellor and other government ministers must uphold the continued independence of the judiciary.

12.4.3 Protection of judicial independence

1. Judges have immunity from being sued for anything they do in the course of their judicial duties (*Sirros v Moore* (1975)).

2. By convention, individual judges are not criticised during parliamentary debates.

3. Judicial salaries are paid from the Consolidated Fund so that payment is made without the need for parliamentary authorisation.

4. The security of tenure of superior judges protects them from the threat of removal by the Government.

12.4.4 Bias

1. Judges are viewed as too pro-establishment and conservative with a small 'c'. Professor Griffiths cites cases such as *Attorney-General v Guardian Newspapers Ltd* (1987) and *R v Secretary of State for the Home Office, ex parte Brind* (1991) to support this view.

2. Natural justice demands that no man be a judge in his own cause. In addition, a judge who is involved, whether personally or as a director of a company, in promoting the same causes as one of the parties to the action, is automatically disqualified from hearing the case (*In Re Pinochet Ugarte* (1999)).

3. The test for bias on the material circumstances of a judge's involvement is an objective test, ie whether or not the fair-minded observer would consider that there was a real danger of bias (*Director General of Fair Trading v The Proprietary Association of Great Britain* (2001)).

12.5 The Lord Chancellor's role

1. The Lord Chancellor is appointed by the Prime Minister and can be dismissed by him at any time. The Lord Chancellor will change with a change of Government.

2. The Lord Chancellor is involved in all three arms of State. He is:
   - a member of Parliament (can sit in either House of Commons of House of Lords);
   - a member of the Cabinet (the executive);
   - involved in the appointment of the judiciary.

3. Under the Constitutional Reform Act 2005, the Lord Chancellor no longer needs to be a lawyer.

4. The Constitutional Reform Act 2005 also provides that the Lord Chancellor can be a member of the House of Lords or the House of Commons. In 2007 Jack Straw became the first Lord Chancellor to sit in the House of Commons.

5. The Lord Chancellor is also Minister of Justice. This Ministry was created in 2007 and has responsibility for a large number of justice areas including the courts, tribunals, the Community Legal Service, prisons and the probation service.

13

Lay people in the legal system

Lay magistrates	Juries
• 18 to 65 on appointment • Can sit to age 70	• 18–70
• Live in or near the Justice area • Possess six key qualities • Some people are not eligible, eg those with a criminal conviction, bankrupts, members of the forces and police	• Be on electoral register of area covered by court • Have resided in UK for five years since 13th birthday • Those with certain criminal convictions are disqualified
• Nominated or apply • Interviewed by local advisory committee • Appointed by Lord Chancellor	• Selected at random
• Given training and appraised	• Some are shown video of court – no other training
• Sit in Magistrates' Court • Bench of two or three • Hear summary and triable either way cases • Also do some civil cases • Specially trained magistrates sit in Youth Court	• Sit in Crown Court • Panel of 12 • Hear indictable and triable either way cases • Can be used in some civil cases eg defamation in the High Court or County Court
• Decide verdict • If defendant is guilty also decide sentence	• Decide verdict • Judge decides sentence • In civil cases decide amount of damages

13.1 Lay magistrates

13.1.1 Qualifications

1. On appointment a person must be between 18 and 65 years of age. Since 2004 there has been a policy of appointing some younger magistrates, in their twenties, where suitable.

2. They must live in or near the justice area to which they are appointed.

3. Those with a criminal conviction, undischarged bankrupts, members of the forces, police officers and traffic wardens are not eligible.

4. In 1998 the Lord Chancellor set out six key qualities which candidates should have. These are:
   - good character;
   - understanding and communication;
   - social awareness;
   - maturity and sound temperament;
   - sound judgement;
   - commitment and reliability.

Those appointed must be prepared to sit at least 26 times (and preferably 35 times) per year.

13.1.2 Appointment

1. Lay magistrates are appointed by the Lord Chancellor on behalf of the Queen.

2. The Lord Chancellor relies on recommendations made to him by local advisory committees.

3. Local groups (political parties, trade unions, chambers of commerce, etc) put suitable candidates forward to the local advisory committees. In addition, the advisory committees can advertise for individuals in the local community to put themselves forward.

4. The local committees interview candidates and recommend suitable people to the Lord Chancellor.

5. In putting forward names the committee must also consider the composition of the local Bench in terms of gender, ethnic origin, occupation and political views. The aim is to keep as good a balance as possible of different types of people.

6. Employers are obliged to give employees time off to sit as lay magistrates (s50 Employment Rights Act 1996).

13.1.3 Composition of the Bench

1. Despite the efforts at getting a good mix of people as lay magistrates, there is still a feeling that magistrates are 'middle-class, middle-aged and middle-minded' as the middle classes are over-represented.

2. Women are well represented, making up half of all lay magistrates.

3. Ethnic minorities are still slightly under-represented, though over the past few years more have been appointed.

4. There has been an effort to recruit disabled people to the Bench and the first blind magistrates were appointed in 1998.

5. Only 4% of lay magistrates are under the age of 40.

13.1.4 Training

1. Under the Lay Magistrates National Training Initiative, newly appointed magistrates have to achieve three basic competencies. These are:
   - managing yourself – focusing on some of the basic aspects of self-management in relation to preparing for court, conduct in court and ongoing learning;
   - working as a member of a team – focusing on the team aspect of decision-making in the Magistrates' Court;
   - making judicial decisions – focusing on impartial and structured decision-making.

2. Each new magistrate keeps a Personal Development Log of their progress and has a mentor (an experienced magistrate) to assist them.

3. During the first two years of the new magistrate sitting in court, between eight and 11 of the sessions will be mentored. In the same period the magistrate is also expected to attend about seven training sessions.

4. Appraisals are held to check whether magistrates have acquired the competencies.

5. This scheme involves practical training 'on the job'. It answers the criticisms of the old system where there was no check on whether

magistrates had actually benefited from training sessions they attended.

13.1.5 Retirement and removal

1. Lay magistrates cannot sit on the Bench to hear cases after the age of 70, but are placed on the supplemental list.

2. Section 11 of the Courts Act 2003 gives the Lord Chancellor power to remove a lay justice for the following reasons:
   - incapacity or misbehaviour;
   - a persistent failure to meet such standards of competence as are prescribed by a direction given by the Lord Chancellor; or
   - where the Lord Chancellor is satisfied that the lay justice is declining or neglecting to take a proper part in the exercise of his functions as a justice of the peace.

3. About ten lay magistrates are removed from office each year.

13.1.6 Role

1. Two or three lay magistrates sit together to form a Bench. They have wide powers over criminal cases. They have jurisdiction to:
   - try all summary offences;
   - sentence those who are guilty (the maximum sentence is six months' imprisonment – 12 months for two offences);
   - deal with mode of trial hearings for all triable either way offences, and try those which it is decided should be dealt with in the Magistrates' Court;
   - deal with the first hearing of all indictable offences and then transfer those cases to the Crown Court;
   - hear applications for bail;
   - issue arrest and search warrants.

2. Specially trained lay magistrates also sit in the Youth Court.

3. Lay magistrates also have jurisdiction to deal with the following civil matters:
   - licensing appeals;
   - enforcing demands for council tax;
   - family cases.

4. Each Bench is assisted by a Magistrates' Clerk who guides the magistrates on questions of law, practice and procedure.

13.1.7 Advantages

1. There is involvement of lay people with local knowledge.

2. Having three magistrates on a panel is likely to give a balanced view.

3. Magistrates come from a greater cross-section of society than professional judges.

4. As they are only paid expenses, the system is cheaper than using professional judges.

5. Improved training and appraisal should improve the quality of the Bench.

13.1.8 Disadvantages

1. There is a much higher conviction rate in the Magistrates' Court than in the Crown Court. This leads to allegations of bias in favour of the police and prosecution.

2. There is not a balanced cross-section of society as the middle classes are over-represented on the Bench.

3. There is inconsistency in sentencing.

4. There is inconsistency in granting of bail.

5. Lay magistrates lack legal knowledge and may rely too heavily on the clerk.

13.2 Juries

13.2.1 Use of juries

1. Juries are used in criminal cases in the Crown Court where the defendant pleads not guilty.

2. There is limited use of juries in civil cases in the High Court and County Court. The only civil cases in which there is a right to jury trial are defamation, false imprisonment, malicious prosecution and fraud.

3. Juries are used in the Coroners' Court to inquire into deaths occurring in or where a police officer is involved or which occurred in certain accidents.

13.2.2 Jury qualifications

1. The basic qualifications are laid down by the Juries Act 1974. These are that to serve on a jury a person must:
   - be aged between 18 and 70;
   - be registered as a parliamentary or local government elector;
   - have been resident in the UK for at least five years since their thirteenth birthday.

2. In addition, people are disqualified from jury service if they:
   - have been sentenced to life imprisonment or a custodial sentence of five years or more;
   - have served any other custodial sentence or received a suspended prison sentence within the last ten years;
   - have been subject to a community order within the last ten years;
   - are currently on bail.

3. Some categories of people used to be ineligible to serve on a jury. These included the Judiciary and others who have been concerned in the administration of justice within the last ten years.

4. Some people used to have the right to be excused from jury service. These included:
   - those over the age of 65;
   - Members of Parliament;
   - members of the medical professions;
   - members of the forces.

5. Jury ineligibility has been abolished by the Criminal Justice Act 2003. Judges and others in the administration of justice are now eligible for jury service.

6. In *R v Abdroikov* (2007) the House of Lords considered three cases in which police or others working in the administration of justice had sat as jurors. The Lords decided that the most important principle was that 'justice had to be seen to be done'. They held:
   - the fact that a police officer was on the jury did not make a trial automatically unfair;
   - however, where the officer on the jury worked from the same police station as police giving evidence against the defendant, then this meant that justice was not being seen to be done;
   - allowing a senior Crown Prosecutor for the area to sit on a jury also meant that justice was not being seen to be done.

7. Mentally disordered persons are exempt from service.

8. Excusal as of right has been abolished by the Criminal Justice Act 2003. MPs, doctors and other medical staff will no longer be able to refuse to do jury service, though they can ask for a discretionary excusal.

9. Once summonsed for jury service it is possible to apply for discretionary excusal. This will only be granted if there is good reason, such as being too ill to attend. Jury service can also be deferred where the date given is inconvenient, eg because of examinations or business commitments.

13.2.3 Selection of a jury panel

1. Names are selected at random from the electoral register for the area in which the court is situated. The selection is done by computer at the Central Summoning Bureau.

2. Those names chosen may be vetted for criminal convictions via the police computer data of criminal records.

3. In exceptional cases, a juror's background and political affiliation may be vetted. This should only occur in cases involving national security or terrorism. The Attorney-General must give permission for vetting (Practice Note (Jury: Stand by: Jury Checks) (1988)).

4. At court both prosecution and defence can challenge individual jurors for cause (s12 Juries Act 1974).

5. There may also be a challenge to the array, ie the whole jury panel, on the basis that it was chosen in an unrepresentative and biased way (s5 Juries Act 1974).

6. However, the fact that a jury does not contain any ethnic minority jurors is not a ground for challenge (*R v Ford* (1989)).

7. The prosecution may stand by individual jurors without giving a reason, but this right should be used sparingly (Practice Note (Jury: Stand by: Jury Checks) (1988)).

8. The judge may discharge any juror whom he thinks lacks the capacity to act effectively as a juror (s9 Juries Act 1974).

13.2.4 Problems with selection

1. Not all people, especially the young and ethnic minorities, are registered to vote. The use of the electoral register excludes these. It also excludes homeless people.

2. Although the selection is random, this may not produce a cross-section of society.

3. There are too many discretionary excusals – Ministry of Justice research found that in 2005 only 64 per cent of those summoned served as jurors. This further undermines the representativeness of the jury.

4. Vetting is considered an invasion of privacy, but the Court of Appeal has ruled that it is lawful (*R v Mason* (1980), *R v McCann* (1990)).

13.2.5 The role of the jury in criminal cases

1. A jury is used in less than 2% of criminal cases.

2. There is a split function between the judge and the jury. The jury decides the facts and the judge decides the law.

3. The jury decides the verdict of guilty or not guilty. If the defendant is found guilty, the judge decides the sentence.

4. The judge cannot place pressure on the jury (*Bushell's* case (1670), *R v McKenna* (1960)).

5. The jury's verdict can be unanimous or, after at least two hours' deliberation, by a majority of 10 to 2 or 11 to 1.

6. Where the verdict is by majority, s17(3) Juries Act 1974 states that the foreman of the jury must state in court the number agreeing and the number disagreeing with the verdict. However, the Court of Appeal has held that, provided the number agreeing with verdict is within the allowed majority, there is no need for the foreman to state also how many disagreed (*R v Pigg* (1983)).

13.2.6 Advantages of juries

1. There is public involvement in the legal system which makes the system more open.

2. The defendant is tried by his peers.

3. There is public confidence in the use of juries.

4. They are 'the lamp that shows that freedom lives' (Lord Devlin).

5. The use of 12 jurors should cancel out any individual bias.

6. The jury is independent. This allows the members to come to a 'just' verdict as opposed to a 'legal' verdict (*Ponting's* case (1985), *R v Randle and Pottle* (1991)).

13.2.7 Disadvantages of juries

1. The jury's decision is reached in secret. The reasons for that decision are not known.

2. In some cases the jury has used unreliable means of coming to a decision, eg in *R v Young* (1991), where a ouija board was used to contact the dead victims.

3. Jurors may be racially biased, as in *Sander v United Kingdom* (2000) where the European Court of Human Rights ruled that a jury should have been discharged.

4. The House of Lords has ruled that discussions in the jury room must remain secret and disclosure, even where it showed a problem, could not be allowed to affect a verdict once the verdict had been given (*R v Connor; R v Mirza* (2004)).

5. Jurors may not be able to understand complicated cases. There is provision in the Criminal Justice Act 2003 for complex fraud cases to be tried by a judge alone but this provision will only become law if both Houses of Parliament approve any regulations made for it.

6. Media coverage may influence a jury's verdict, especially in high-profile cases.

7. The compulsory nature of jury service is unpopular.

8. Jurors can be 'nobbled'. In *R v Twomey* (2009), the Court of Appeal (under powers in s44 of the Criminal Justice Act 2003) made the first order that a trial should be held by a judge alone, after earlier trials had collapsed because of attempts to 'nobble' the jury.

9. Acquittal rates in the Crown Court are criticised for being too high. However, a large number of acquittals are directed by the judge. The jury acquits in about 36% of cases.

10. The use of a jury makes a case longer and more expensive.

13.2.8 Special problems of civil juries

1. In civil cases the jury decides the issue of liability and also the amount of damages to be paid.

2. Civil juries may be biased against newspapers or well-known personalities involved in libel cases.

3. The amount of damages is unpredictable and inconsistent. However, on appeal the Court of Appeal can substitute the amount it feels is proper (s8 Courts and Legal Services Act 1990).

4. Juries add very heavily to the costs of the case. The losing party is likely to face a bill of hundreds of thousands of pounds.

13.3 Other lay people in the system

1. Lay members are used in tribunals. These will have knowledge of the type of cases heard by the particular tribunal.

2. Lay members with expert knowledge are also used in some of the specialist courts, such as the Restrictive Practices Court and the Admiralty Court.

14

Legal services and funding

HELP FOR FUNDING

CIVIL CASES

Advice
- Lawyers or advice agencies with a contract
- Website

Representation
- Community Legal Service
- Must show case should be funded
- Must qualify financially
- Some cases not funded, eg personal injury, defamation, claims under £5,000

Private help
- Conditional fee agreements
- Some *pro bono* representation available

CRIMINAL CASES

Advice
- Duty solicitor at police station
- Duty solicitor at Magistrates' Court

Representation
- Criminal Defence Service
- Available if in the interests of justice
- Must qualify financial
- May have salaried defender or private lawyer

Private help
- Must pay full fee
- Conditional fee agreements NOT allowed

14.1 Public funding for civil cases

Under the Access to Justice Act 1999, there are now two schemes. These are the Community Legal Service for civil matters and the Criminal Defence Service for criminal cases. The Legal Services Commission oversees the public funding for both these schemes.

14.1.1 The Community Legal Service

1. The Community Legal Service provides the following services for matters involving civil law:
   - general information about the law and legal system and the availability of legal services;
   - legal advice;
   - help in preventing or otherwise resolving disputes about legal rights and duties (this may include representation in the County Court or the High Court);
   - help in enforcing decisions by which such disputes are resolved.
2. The money to pay for this service comes out of the Community Legal Fund. There is a set limit for the fund.
3. Certain types of civil cases are not funded by the Community Legal Services Fund. These include:
   - claims for personal injury, or death or damage to property through someone else's negligence;
   - defamation or malicious falsehood cases;
   - claims for amounts of less than £5,000;
   - most tribunal hearings, except for cases involving human rights, eg asylum or mental health reviews.

14.1.2 Funding criteria

1. The person must show that their case should be funded. To decide this, the following points are considered:
   - the likely cost of funding and the benefit which may be obtained;
   - the amount of money in the Community Legal Fund;
   - the importance of the matters for the individual;
   - the availability of other services (such as conditional fees);
   - how likely it is that the case will be won; there must be a realistic chance of the case succeeding before public money is made available for it.
2. The person must qualify financially. To decide this, their disposable income and disposable capital are calculated.
3. Disposable income is the amount of income available to a person after taking into account essential living expenses.
4. Disposable capital is the assets owned by the person. It includes the equitable value of the home above £100,000.

5. If disposable income and capital are below the minimum limits, the person will receive free funding. If their disposable income and capital are above the maximum allowed, then they do not qualify for help. If their disposable income and capital are between the minimum and maximum figures they will have to pay a contribution towards the cost of the funding.

6. The limits are quite low, eg anyone with more than £8,000 capital will not qualify.

14.1.3 Problems with funding of civil cases

1. Money is allocated to regional offices of the Commission according to the amount identified as necessary for that area. This could result in one area not having enough to fund all the cases it needs.

2. Very expensive cases are funded on a case-by-case basis through individually negotiated contracts from a central fund.

3. About 2,500 firms of solicitors have contracts. This is less than a third of the number who previously did legal aid work. There are problems of access to justice in some areas where there is no solicitor doing publicly funded work.

4. Even solicitors who do publicly funded work are cutting back on the number of cases they take because of the low rates of pay.

5. The Citizens Advice Bureau reported in 2004 that there were 'advice deserts' in some parts of the country where there were no legal aid solicitors available for important cases such as those involving housing or health law.

6. The statutory charge (clawback) can mean that a claimant has very little left from their damages even though they won the case.

14.2 Private funding for civil cases

Paying privately for a lawyer is very expensive, especially in London. Most individuals who do not qualify for help and representation under the government scheme cannot afford to pay full private fees. For this reason conditional fee agreements have been developed.

14.2.1 Conditional fees

1. These were first allowed by the Courts and Legal Services Act 1990 and extended by the Access to Justice Act 1999.

2. The solicitor and client agree on the fee that would normally be charged for such a case, with a 'success fee' payable if the case is won.

3. If the solicitor does not win the case, then the client pays nothing. If the solicitor is successful then the client pays the normal fee plus the success fee.

4. The Access to Justice Act 1999 allows courts to order that the losing party pays the amount of the success fee to the winning party.

5. It is possible to insure against losing a case and, if the case is won, s29 Access to Justice Act 1999 allows the court to order the losing party to pay the cost of insurance premiums.

14.3 Advice agencies

Free advice can be obtained from a number of agencies. Some of them specialise in a particular area of law, others give general advice. Some examples are:

- the Citizens Advice Bureau;
- law centres;
- the Community Legal Service website;
- the Bar's Free Representation Unit which represents litigants in court.

14.4 The Criminal Defence Service

1. Since April 2001 the Criminal Defence Service has been responsible for the funding of criminal cases for defendants.

2. This service is aimed at 'securing that individuals involved in criminal investigations or proceedings have access to such advice, assistance and representation as the interests of justice require'.

14.4.1 Advice and assistance

1. There is a duty solicitor scheme for people who are arrested and held in custody at a police station. This is free.

2. This is now organised through the Defence Solicitors' Call Centre.

3. When someone is arrested, the custody officer at the police station must tell them about this scheme.

4. Criminal Defence Service Direct provides telephone-only advice for minor matters. But if a suspect is being interviewed by the police they are entitled to have a solicitor present at the interview.

5. There is also a duty solicitor scheme at many Magistrates' Courts for people to receive free advice on their cases. The solicitor may also represent them on matters such as bail applications.

14.4.2 Representation

1. The Legal Services Commission has the power to decide when a defendant should have a legal representative paid for by the State.

2. This is done by deciding if it is in the interests of justice for the defendant to be represented in court. Five categories are considered. These are whether:

   - the individual would, if any matter arising in the proceedings is decided against him, be likely to lose his liberty or livelihood or suffer serious damage to his reputation;
   - the determination of any matter arising in the proceedings may involve consideration of a substantial point of law;
   - the individual may be unable to understand the proceedings or to state his own case;
   - the proceedings may involve the tracing, interviewing or expert cross-examination of witnesses on behalf of the individual;
   - it is in the interests of another person that the individual is represented.

3. Defendants in the magistrates' courts are means tested. They will only qualify for publicly funded representation if they are on a low level of income.

4. During 2010, means testing for Crown Court cases is being brought in. The levels of disposable income and capital are higher than those allowed for Magistrates' Court cases.

14.4.3 Budget

There is no fixed budget and the funding of criminal cases is demand led. If the cost of criminal cases becomes very heavy, then it is possible for funds from the civil budget to be transferred to the criminal budget.

14.4.4 The Public Defender Service

1. The Public Defender Service has salaried lawyers to represent defendants. It initially opened offices in eight areas, but four of them have been closed because they were not financially viable.

2. There is criticism that such a system means that the State is both prosecuting the defendant (through the Crown Prosecution Service) and defending the defendant.

3. There have been criticisms that the Service is more expensive than using lawyers in private practice.

Index